DATE DUE

DE 22 '95			
NO 22 99			
DE 19 01			

Mules and Dragons

MULES AND
Dragons

Popular Culture Images in the Selected Writings of African-American and Chinese-American Women Writers

MARY E. YOUNG

Contributions in Women's Studies, Number 136

GREENWOOD PRESS
Westport, Connecticut • London

Library of Congress Cataloging-in-Publication Data

Young, Mary E.
    Mules and dragons : popular culture images in the selected
writings of African-American and Chinese-American women writers /
Mary E. Young.
        p.   cm.—(Contributions in women's studies, ISSN 0147–104X ;
no. 136)
    Includes bibliographical references and index.
    ISBN 0–313–28735–X (alk. paper)
    1. American literature—Afro-American authors—History and
criticism.   2. American literature—Chinese American authors—
History and criticism.   3. American literature—Women authors—
History and criticism.   4. Stereotype (Psychology) in literature.
5. Women and literature—United States.   6. Popular culture in
literature.   I. Title.   II. Series.
PS153.N5Y64   1993
810.9′9287—dc20   92–45119

British Library Cataloguing in Publication Data is available.

Library of Congress Catalog Card Number: 92–45119
ISBN: 0–313–28735–X
ISSN: 0147–104X

First published in 1993

Greenwood Press, 88 Post Road West, Westport, CT 06881
An imprint of Greenwood Publishing Group, Inc.

Printed in the United States of America

The paper used in this book complies with the
Permanent Paper Standard issued by the National
Information Standards Organization (Z39.48–1984).

10 9 8 7 6 5 4 3 2 1

To Courtney

Contents

Preface

The motivation to tackle this topic was the realization that most stereotypes of women of color are inaccurate as well as malicious. As an African-American woman who has lived, worked, and traveled in East Asia, I have found that the stereotypes are far from reality. Therefore, the intent of this study has been to compare and to contrast not only the histories of two groups, African-American women and Chinese-American women, but also each group's response to the stereotyped images that have become part of American cultural history.

These two groups were chosen rather than other groups of women because of the similarities between them. Both groups were at one time denied United States citizenship, and both had popular culture images that branded them as immoral. This unique stereotyping of African-American women and Chinese-American women as immoral has set them apart from other groups of women. Native American women, Hispanic women, and Jewish women have also been stereotyped, but none of the stereotypes of these women has been as persistent, pervasive, or pernicious as the stereotypes of African-American and Chinese-American women.

In their writings, I was seeking an artistic expression of these two groups' experiences in the United States, principally responses to the stereotypes. However, in choosing authors to study, I was limited by the writings available. As a result, the African-American writers explored here reflect my personal tastes since few fail to mention the effect of the stereotypes that arose from a racist society had on their group. However,

Chinese-American women writers have not published as long or as consistently as African-American women.

Finally, some acknowledgments are important. Barbara Hampton took
a rather rambling manuscript and gave it structure and organization.
Darren Floyd, my research assistant, discovered important, interesting,
and relevant data, Gerald Horne was always available with encouragement
and advice, and the College of Wooster gave me much-needed financial
support for the final revisions. I willingly take responsibility for any factual
errors or overstatements that remain.

Chapter One

"John Chinaman" as "Sambo"

Most Americans would claim at least a superficial knowledge of African-American history, which would undoubtedly include slavery and Emancipation. But since little Asian-American history is taught, most Americans would not acknowledge holding cursory information about Chinese-Americans. African-American women authors from Linda Brent to Alice Walker have confronted their history by acknowledging it, incorporating certain aspects into their writing, and challenging the assumptions that have arisen from it. But the history of Chinese-Americans is seldom included in the writings of Chinese-American women, although their history and images are intertwined with those of African-Americans. A study of these writings demonstrates the development of a mythic Chinese past rather than an American reality.

On July 13, 1869, approximately six years after Emancipation, a group of Southern planters met in Memphis[1] to explore possible solutions to their labor problem and, concomitantly, their problem with the freedman. The recently freed slaves were voting, running for and being elected to office, demanding equal pay for work, and no longer limiting themselves to agricultural work. The Southern planters were meeting to consider putting a plan into action that would return the now-unmanageable freedman into his former enslaved position. The planters had considered introducing another racial group to do the work formerly done by the ex-slaves, probably eastern or southern Europeans, but this plan did not receive sufficient support. In the end, the planters finally approved a scheme "aimed at preserving the traditional Southern labor system by substituting

Chinese hands"[2] for the ex-slaves. With their reputation as industrious and hard working, the Chinese would be used to teach the ex-slaves the work skills that African-Americans were purportedly lacking. If the plan had worked, the planters would have had two groups from which to choose workers to perform labor formerly only done by one—African slaves.

Many Chinese laborers had completed work on the Trans-Continental Railroad and were available for recruitment into the South. The Chinese Labor Convention, as the Memphis convention came to be called, finally agreed to import Chinese "coolie"[3] labor either from California or directly from China into the South, although many Chinese came from Cuba, Peru, or other parts of Central and South America. There was a certain logic associated with the plan. Wherever slavery had been abolished, Chinese "coolie" labor followed. "The great outward movement of coolie labor that followed in the years 1845 to 1877 was a direct consequence of the discontinuance of slavery in the British Empire."[4] In 1833 Great Britain abolished slavery, and in 1838 slavery was abolished in the West Indies. Each instance of the abolition of African slavery in the British Empire or the Spanish Empire was followed by an outward flow of Chinese labor. A similar movement of Chinese labor following the abolition of African slavery is also observable in the Spanish colonies. The abolition of African slavery in Colombia (1851), Venezuela (1854), Ecuador (1852), and Chile (1823) was followed by small groups of Chinese laborers, but large contingents of Chinese arrived in Peru (1851), Cuba (1886), and Mexico (1828). Chinese arrived in Mexico in such numbers that the Mexican traditional dress is referred to as *La China Poblana*, the Chinese Pueblan girl.

However, although the convention expected to import thousands of Chinese, "only a trickle of Chinese found their way into the South."[5] Those Chinese who did come performed traditional slave labor. They worked in the cotton, cane, rice, and sugar fields. The plan failed for any number of reasons "even with the added inducement of 1/2 lb. of opium monthly"[6] in addition to the regular wages. The probable reason was that the traditional inhumane treatment of the slaves was expanded to encompass the Chinese. Many of the Chinese failed to live up to the terms of their contracts as indentured workers; unlike slaves, they felt free to leave at any opportune time.

When they broke their contracts, many of the Chinese returned to the work that they had previously performed—building railroads. They worked on portions of the Alabama and Chattanooga Railroad and the Houston and Texas Railroad. After they had completed their work on the railroad, many remained in the South. Entering a biracial society composed of African-Americans and Euro-Americans, the Chinese were automatically designated "colored."[7]

In Mississippi the Chinese who remained after the completion of their contracts or after breaking their contracts were "considered . . . to be of roughly Negro status and [were] barred . . . from white schools, organizations, and other social interaction."[8] As "colored" people, the Chinese had to adhere to a Jim Crow system that now became a tripartite structure to accommodate the Chinese. Many Mississippi communities maintained separate schools and cemeteries for the Chinese, in addition to those maintained for African-Americans. Those Chinese who could find no other employment opened small grocery stores that serviced African-American areas, frequently living over their stores or behind them. Because laws prevented the immigration of Chinese women or cohabitation with Euro-American women,[9] Chinese men were assumed to be celibate. However, many of them did establish relations with African-American women.[10] These relations produced offspring who were referred to by the dominant society as Chinese-Negroes.[11] This cohabitation with African-American women and their subsequent children reinforced their "colored" designation.

Many Chinese did not accept their classification as "colored" for several reasons. A "colored" designation would force their children to attend African-American schools, which they considered inferior.[12] Neither did they "wish to be assimilated or amalgamated into the black culture or race."[13] Somehow the Chinese had to be recognized as a group distinctly different from African-Americans. One of the means available to change their racial status was the use of the legal system. In 1924 Gong Lum sued the state of Mississippi, demanding that his daughter be allowed to attend the Euro-American school rather than the African-American school to which she had been assigned. His argument that "the white race creates for itself a privilege that it denies to other races; exposes the children of other races to the risks and dangers to which it would not expose its own children"[14] was rejected by the state supreme court. The court asserted that Chinese "are not 'white' and must fall under the heading 'colored' races."[15]

Unable to continue to accept their classification as "colored," the Mississippi Chinese sought other means of improving their situation. Representatives of the Chinese community approached the Euro-American majority to find possible solutions to their problems.[16] Among several suggestions that the Euro-Americans offered were that the Chinese convert to Christianity, make financial contributions to Euro-American organizations, disassociate themselves from the African-American community, and establish no liaisons with Euro-American women.[17] The Chinese agreed and ostracized those members of the community who refused to abandon their African-American families.[18] The accommodations made by the Chinese were based on what they perceived as Euro-American cultural objectives and a desire to alter their image to become more acceptable to Euro-Americans.[19] After complying with the suggested changes, Loewen writes in *The Mississippi Chinese*, the Chinese "became white" with the addition of the " 'W' in the appropriate blank on their driver's license."[20] To demonstrate their allegiance and adherence to Euro-American standards, "in the presence of whites, they . . . would joke about blacks, telling whites of the Cantonese derogatory term for 'nigger.' "[21]

In areas where the Chinese population was small, the change of race, and thus social status, for the Chinese was not rare. The Chinese as second-class white citizens were becoming more acceptable within some Euro-American communities. "In the Midwest and Southern states . . . the Chinese are classified as 'white.' "[22] But for those Chinese who lived on the West Coast, particularly California, the situation was quite different.

Establishing similarities between the Chinese and African-Americans had begun before the Chinese arrived in California following the gold rush of 1849. British writer Sir John Barrow in *Travels in China* (1803) noted several physical similarities between Chinese and Hottentots.[23] Barrow cited physical similarities as well as voice, manner of speaking, temperament, and mental qualities.[24] Other writers traveling in Africa and Asia mentioned similar qualities.[25] In the United States, Hinton Helper in *Land of Gold* (1855) equated the immigration of the Chinese to the West Coast with the existence of African-Americans in the South and East. "Helper's comparison between the two groups prefigured a stereotyping process: the Chinese were associated with Blacks in the racial imagination of Euro-American society."[26] Thus, the "negroization" of the Chinese was initiated, although the process was very carefully fabricated. Apparently every stereotype that was used against African-Americans was now used against the Chinese, beginning with the image of slave.

After 1865 the activities of the "coolie" trade came under more careful scrutiny. Among the many comparisons of the African slave trade to the "coolie" trade was the image of the "Middle Passage" (for slaves, the trip across the Atlantic) in the Chinese voyage to the United States. Stuart Creighton Miller writes in *The Unwelcome Immigrant* that "descriptions of coolies suffocating in crammed quarters on 'slave decks,' being burned to death or drowned in nautical catastrophes, and committing suicide or staging desperate and bloody mutinies conjured up all the horrors of the old 'middle passage.' "[27]

By the 1870s the subject of continuing, limiting, or prohibiting Chinese immigration had become a national issue. "In the congressional debates over Chinese immigration . . . the issue of slavery was preeminent."[28] During these debates, Chinese immigration was frequently alluded to as a modern slave trade system. According to these exchanges, the Chinese were not voluntary immigrants but were captured and assembled in China and sold in various ports in the Western Hemisphere. C. E. De Long, a former ambassador to Japan, speaking for an enlightened majority, said, "These coolies are more absolute slaves that ever the negroes [sic] of the South were."[29]

The analogy of the Chinese to African slaves was widespread throughout the United States. The Chinese worked in labor gangs, which reminded many Americans of African slave gangs, which in turn reinforced the image of slavery.[30] But they were not to be completely confused with the African slaves because at the time slavery was illegal. However, the Chinese had been recruited into a "slavery not of law but of condition and custom."[31] Terry Boswell, writing in *The American Sociological Review,* has alleged that even the "low-cost Chinese labor was considered a type of slavery. Chinese immigrants were accused of being slaves to gang bosses, to capitalists, and even to the Emperor of China."[32]

The year 1877 was a critical juncture in both anti-Chinese legislation and anti-African-American legislation. After his election to the presidency in 1877 to the presidency, Rutherford B. Hayes induced Congress to allow individual states to solve the "Negro Problem." To assist the South in finding its own solutions, federal troops were withdrawn. Now the South could deal with African-Americans on its own terms without fear of federal intervention or reprisals. The restriction and persecution of the Chinese was extensively related to the restriction and persecution of African-Americans.

Before the Civil War many Southerners had moved to California with their slaves. Along with their slaves they brought their racist attitudes. "California was made a white man's state by the Constitution of 1849. Article 2, section 1 dealing with citizenship begins with these words 'Every white male citizen,' and the Constitution of 1879 reiterated this, strengthening it by specially mentioning Mongolians as ineligible to citizenship."[33] There were many Southerners in California in addition to those Southern Democrats who dominated its politics, rendering anyone who was not of European heritage suspect. The abrogation of civil rights on the national level was the result of Democrats' and Republicans' attempting to pacify California by concurring on the Chinese question. So the Naturalization Act of 1870 gave citizenship rights to African-Americans but not to the Chinese. The act specified that only "free whites" and "African aliens" were eligible for naturalization. This was not an arguable point since the question of Chinese racial identity had been established as early as 1854 when Chan Young unsuccessfully applied for citizenship. Chan's application was refused because he was not "free white" or an "African alien."

Additional legislation was enacted to oppress and circumscribe further the Chinese in the United States just as the law had been used in the isolation and oppression of African-Americans. Many of these laws intended to draw the Chinese into the Jim Crow system. The law that confirmed the "negroization" of the Chinese was *People v. Hall* in 1854. An earlier California statute had stated that "no black or mulatto person, or Indian, shall be permitted to give evidence in favor of, or against, any white person."[34] The question in *People v. Hall* was whether these restrictions included the Chinese. The U.S. Supreme Court reversed Hall's conviction, which relied heavily on the testimony of Chinese witnesses, declaring that the words "Indian, Negro, Black, and White were generic terms, designating races, and that therefore Chinese and other people not white could not testify against whites."[35] According to Dan Caldwell, this ruling gave the Chinese the same status as Native Americans and African-Americans so that "for all legal purposes the Chinese had become a Negro."[36] Even before the legal machinery had been set in motion to equate the Chinese with African-Americans, Chinese migrants discovered that stereotypical racial characteristics that had been assigned to African-Americans rapidly developed into Chinese characteristics. Ronald Takaki, author of *Strangers from a Different Shore*, the first inclusive history of Asian-Americans, asserts that "white workers referred to the Chinese as 'nagurs,' "[37] and a cartoon included in Dan Caldwell's "The Negroization of the Chinese Stereotype in California" depicts the Chinese as vampires with black skin, slanted eyes, and thick lips.[38] Like African-Americans, the Chinese were described in the media as well as in popular fiction as pagan, morally inferior, barbaric, childlike, and wanton. The Chinese were considered alternatives or substitutes for African slave labor and were treated accordingly in their daily lives, in newspapers, such as the *New York Courier* and the *New York Tribune*, in magazines, including the *Missionary Review of the World*, and the *American Catholic Quarterly*, and in the courts.

Because of this paralleling of Chinese with African-Americans, Jim Crow laws that were designed for African-Americans were expanded to include the Chinese. "Jim Crow" is from the name of a song sung by Thomas Rice in a minstrel show that eventually became synonymous with

"Black." By 1901 Jim Crow was an important part of the American scene, requiring complete separation of the races. According to Lerone Bennett, the motivation was fear "from economic competition and political needs, from frustration, from an obsession with the cult of White Womanhood. In only two other countries—South Africa and Nazi Germany—have men's fears driven them to such extremes."[39] The same laws that applied to African-Americans also applied to the Chinese, who were not permitted to eat in certain restaurants, sit on the first floor in movie theaters, or live in certain neighborhoods outside Chinatown.

In 1860 Chinese children were refused admission to public schools. After 1866, many were allowed to attend these schools only if Euro-American parents did not object. Although by 1885 *Tape v. Hurley* decided that the Chinese could not be refused admission to public schools, segregation of the Chinese in the public school system lasted until 1946, and in some cases until *Brown v. Board of Education* ended public school segregation in 1954. The Chinese were not admitted to most public hospitals. Chinese were denied admission to San Francisco City Hospital, and it was only in 1925 that a Chinese hospital was built.[40] California state law stipulated that no Chinese could be hired by state, county, or municipal governments for public works.

By 1882 animosity toward the Chinese had increased to the level that the Chinese Exclusion Act was passed, which banned the immigration of Chinese laborers for ten years. The act additionally provided that anyone unqualified for citizenship could not enter the country—and by the terms of the 1870 Naturalization Act, Chinese were not eligible for citizenship. In 1884, a federal court ruling interpreted the provisions of the 1882 act to confirm the prohibition against the immigration of the wives of Chinese laborers. This law had international repercussions for the Chinese. Anti-Chinese or exclusion laws were passed by Natal (1897), Orange Free State (1899), Australia (1901), the Cape of Good Hope (1904), Transvaal (1907), New Zealand (1920), and Canada (1923). But American citizenship for *any* Chinese was still problematic. Previous attempts to obtain citizenship had been thwarted by the judicial system. It was only in 1896 in *United States v. Wong Kim Ark* that it was decided that a person born in the United States to Chinese parents is an American.

The Chinese were learning to use the legal system to their advantage. In 1880 San Francisco enacted an ordinance making it illegal for any person to establish or carry on a laundry within the corporate limits of the city and the county. Under this statute all petitions of laundrymen who had wooden buildings but were not Chinese were granted. Yick Wo, a San Francisco laundryman for twenty years, continued to operate his business without a license, but eventually he was arrested and found guilty of violating the ordinance.[41] Yick Wo took his case to the United States Supreme Court in 1896. The Court reversed the San Francisco safety ordinances, saying that they were indeed designed to harass laundrymen of Chinese ancestry.[42]

Although the Civil Rights Act of 1875 provided that all persons within the jurisdiction of the United States were entitled to equal treatment under the law, including public accommodations, "subject only to the conditions and limitations established by law and applicable alike to citizens of every race and color, regardless of any previous condition of servitude," California methodically supported discriminatory policies against the Chinese until 1924, when the federal government succeeded in excluding all Asian nationalities. From fear of unfair competition, labor unions and miners' organizations, many under the leadership of Dennis Kearney,[43] significantly affected the nature of state and federal legislation concerning immigration by writing slanted newspaper articles and lobbying local, state, and federal legislatures.

Regardless of the images constructed by the dominant society, Jack Chen insists in *The Chinese of America* that "the only [Chinese] slaves were the women kidnapped and brought to America to be prostitutes, often with the connivance of the courts and the immigration authorities."[44] However, more direct evidence of the nature of Chinese slavery is in Charles Frederick Holder's "Chinese Slavery in America" in the September 1897 edition of the *North American Review*.

It seems incredible that slavery should be boldly advocated and carried on with all the elaboration and system that characterize any successful commercial project. . . . [There is in San Francisco] an apartment known as the "Queen's Room," in reality a public slave mart, where the victims were brought and exhibited to dealers and would-be purchasers. . . . The girls . . . are valued at from $150 to $3,500. . . . The girl is . . . on exhibition for sale, and is critically examined by highbinders, slave-dealers, speculators, brothel keepers, and others interested in the sale.[45]

Corresponding to Holder's description of a Chinese slave market, Kenneth Stampp describes an African slave market for prospective prostitutes: "Lewis C. Robards . . . had special quarters . . . for his 'choice stock.' . . . Prospective purchasers usually examined the trader's merchandise minutely."[46] In the minds of most Americans in the nineteenth century, the view of the Chinese as slaves, especially the women, was as great as the view of the Africans as slaves.

The negative image of African-American women predates the founding of the United States. English slave traders described African women as "hot constitution'd ladies, possessed of a lascivious temper, with an inclination for White men."[47] This image sanctioned the exploitation of African-American women in addition to holding them responsible for the alleged actions of African-American men. Paula Giddings posits that

the stereotype of the sexually potent Black male was largely based on that of the promiscuous Black female. He would have to be potent . . . to satisfy such hot-natured women. Now released from the constraints of White masters, the Black man found White women so "alluring" and "seductive" because . . . of the wantonness of the women of his own race.[48]

An equal image was created for Chinese women. It was commonly accepted that they all were prostitutes and would degrade any who came in contact with them. Frank Pixley expressed this attitude when he wrote, "I believe . . . of the multitudes of Chinese women in our state there is not a wife or virtuous female in their number."[49]

Although African-American women have been censured for their alleged lack of morality, the accusations did not reach the level of those aimed at Chinese women. Ulysses S. Grant said in his annual address of 1874:

Hardly a perceptible percentage of them perform any honorable labor, but they are brought for shameful purposes, to the great demoralization of the youth of these localities. If this evil practice can be legislated against, it will be my pleasure as well as my duty to enforce any regulation to secure so desirable an end.[50]

Caving in to public pressure, Congress passed the Page Law in 1875. Although designed to prevent the importation of "coolie" labor into this country, the law also was aimed at preventing the entrance of *any* Chinese woman into the United States. It was now a felony for a citizen to take to or from the United States any citizen of any Asian country without his or her consent, for the purpose of holding him or her for a term of service. It was also a felony for any person to transport or to keep women for immoral purposes. Any person brought into this country as a prostitute or laborer would be in "violation of this act or of the coolie act of 1862."[51] Although seemingly aimed at women of any race or nationality who would be brought into the United States for prostitution, the law specifically targeted Chinese women. Therefore, United States public policy had the effect of being designed to prevent the entrance of Chinese women into the country. "To prohibit entry of prostitutes was enforced so strictly and broadly it served not only to exclude Chinese prostitutes but also discourage Chinese wives from coming here."[52]

Those Chinese women already present in the United States were virtual sex slaves. "In the 1870 census . . . 61 percent of the 3,536 Chinese women in California had occupations listed as prostitute."[53] Magazines and newspapers continually published articles depicting the Chinese women as prostitutes and slaves.[54] However, one article was unique. Just as African-American women were used as breeders to increase the owner's stock and wealth, a writer in *Lippincott's Magazine* proposed mating Chinese women with Euro-American men for future workers in California, using the multiracial climate of Hawaii as an example.[55] The view of Chinese women as slaves was widely reported. The *New York Times*, using news dispatches from California newspapers, seemly accepted it as a fact that Chinese women, like African-American women in the antebellum South, were publicly auctioned in California.[56]

As the Ku Klux Klan and similar organizations worked to terrorize African-Americans into maintaining their subordinate status within United States society, similar activities were carried out against the Chinese. Drivings-out began with the passage of the Exclusion Act, not only in California but in most other Western states, where "railroad building was still in process and small settlements of miners remained."[57] These terrorist activities were commonly used to intimidate African-Americans and enforce a social etiquette that could be used to keep African-Americans in "their places." Similar activities were used against the Chinese for similar purposes.

Unlike African-American men, who were targets of terrorist activities because they supposedly raped Euro-American women, Chinese men became targets because of a fear of unfair economic competition. Chinese were lynched, dynamited, and burned out of their homes in cities and towns all over the West. In Rock Springs, Wyoming, in September 1885, more than twenty Chinese were murdered, and hundreds were burned out of their homes. Chinese were put on boxcars and shipped out of Tacoma, Washington, after unruly mobs had burned Chinatown. Federal troops were sent into Seattle, Washington, numerous lynchings of Chinese were reported in Idaho, and in Oregon Chinatowns were dynamited.[58] Up and down the West Coast, Euro-American workingmen were organizing in opposition to the alleged unfair labor competition of the Chinese.

Perhaps the most virulent terrorist activities that stemmed from the organized labor movement occurred in California. In Los Angeles there had been an ongoing feud between two rival groups of Chinese, which resulted in the murder of one of the group members. On October 24, 1871, police intervention in a subsequent melee led to the wounding of two officers. Groups of Euro-Americans hearing of the confrontation rushed into "the Chinese quarter, firing into houses, hanging those whom they caught alive, and appropriating all movable property. The entire affair lasted only four hours, but in that time at least eighteen persons were killed, several buildings were burned, and a large amount of loot was carried away."[59]

These activities were not confined to the West Coast. In Milwaukee, Wisconsin, in 1889, a Chinese laundry was demolished by an angry mob of two thousand people after its two owners were indicted for violating more than twenty Euro-American adolescents between the ages of nine and thirteen in the back room.[60] The *New York Times* reported that in 1883 in Waynesboro, Georgia, townsmen ran the "rat-eaters" out of town.[61] Not all of the terrorist activities were conducted by mobs. In Cleveland in 1925 in response to a murder, the police acted as a mob:

Practically the entire available police force was put to work "cleaning up" Chinatown. Chinese laundrymen were pulled from behind their ironing boards; waiters and patrons of eating places were taken from their tables. The Chinese population of the city was dragged to the police stations. Pedestrians were taken up on the sidewalks, even students at Cleveland institutions of learning were swept up.[62]

Many African-Americans were lynched because they purportedly lusted after Euro-American women. The same charges were made against Chinese men, who were seen as lascivious animals with a particular fondness for Euro-American women.

Scribner's Monthly and other leading magazines of the era recommended that Euro-American women never leave their daughters alone with the Chinese servants because they induced innocent Euro-American women into Chinatown and turned them into drug-abusing prostitutes.[63] Although proselytizing in the Chinese community was common among Protestants, missionaries were warned by parishioners that the Chinese probably attended Sunday School to "debauch their white, female teachers."[64] "In Brooklyn two seventeen year old prostitutes claimed that Chinese laundrymen had started them on their 'shameful life' at a very tender age."[65]

Yet, Chinese men were, despite anti-miscegenation laws, marrying Euro-American women, particularly Irish immigrant women. The October 3, 1857, edition of *Harpers Weekly* reported that "twenty-eight of these . . . women have gone the way of matrimony with their elephant-eyed, olive-skinned contemporaries."[66] This is an interesting phenomenon because the most virulent leaders in the anti-Chinese movement were the Irish, led by Dennis Kearney. Still, the marriages between Chinese men and Irish women were puzzling to the anonymous author of the article, who mused, "But the amalgamation of the Irish and the Chinese is more than bewildering—it begets a chaos of ideas from which no ray of intelligibility can be safely eliminated."[67]

An additional area of comparison between Blacks and Chinese is housing. African-Americans were prevented from moving into certain urban and suburban areas because of restrictive covenants or fear of persecution by the dominant group, which considered their presence objectionable. Similar restrictive covenants used against the Chinese were in effect, for example, in San Francisco until 1964.[68] However, Chinatown has commonly been described as an ethnic enclave, where the Chinese congregate to maintain their cultural integrity. Frank Chin, the first Chinese-American to have a play produced on Broadway, denies that, claiming instead, "The railroads created a detention camp and called it 'Chinatown.' The details of that creation have been conveniently forgotten or euphemized into a state of sweet confusion . . . no one will know it was not us that created a game preserve for Chinese and called it 'Chinatown.' "[69] It has been proposed by other writers, although not as bluntly as Chin, that the popular image of the creation of Chinatown is complete fabrication. Ronald Takaki does confirm that Chinatown is "a ghetto. . . . [It] confirmed views of the Chinese as unhealthy, unassimilable, and undesirable immigrants."[70]

The Chinese were confined to a particular district in most major urban areas of the United States. The Chinese, like the African-Americans, were barred by violence and local ordinances from working and living in the city except as servants. "These were not like the immigrant ghettos of Italians, Jews, or Poles, which tended to disappear as each group integrated into American society. Rather, they were segregated areas where the Chinese were meant to stay,"[71] Peter Kwong noted.

The typical view of the early Chinatown was an area filled with vice: opium dens, gambling parlors, and prostitutes. This image of Chinatown lasted until approximately 1938, when Chinatown was consciously remodeled in the image of a Hollywood Chinese city. Ivan Light, writing in the *Pacific Historical Review*, stated,

Chinatown chambers of commerce began to regulate the architecture on main thoroughfares so that a uniform, pagoda-styled decor replaced ramshackled predecessors. They built Chinatown to suit the taste and imagination of the . . .

American public. . . . The tiered gates of New Chinatown originally graced the movie set of *The Good Earth*, a Hollywood China epic.[72]

Thus, as Light and others have inferred, the congregation of the Chinese into these urban ghettos was not voluntary but was necessary to satisfy customary practice and maintain racial harmony.

There were other areas in which the Chinese paralleled African-Americans. In both groups, choices of occupations were limited. African-Americans were relegated to the most menial, undesirable, back-breaking occupations—construction workers, cooks, and waiters—mostly in the service sector. Laundries and restaurants were two of the very few opportunities open to Chinese. In a narrow, racially restricted labor market, Takaki estimates that "one out of four employed Chinese males in the United States in 1900 was a laundryman."[73]

Both groups allegedly were unable to master standard English. African-Americans speak a legitimate form of English frequently referred to by linguists as "Black English." The usage of this English dialect has been manipulated to brand African-Americans as less intelligent than Euro-Americans. The supposed inability of the Chinese to speak English has been part of the stereotyping process. The Chinese, and indeed all Asians, allegedly confuse *l*'s and *r*'s, add an extra vowel consisting of double *e*'s to the ends of words and usually omit most articles and the verb "to be." Additionally, in the manner of Charlie Chan, the Chinese were thought to use many pseudo-Confucian aphorisms.

Both groups were accused of having strong animal-like smells. In Massachusetts in 1876 "one English language teacher reported that her health had been broken by the smell of her Chinese students."[74] There were other areas in which the dominant culture made very deliberate attempts to "negroicize" the Chinese.[75]

Despite the machinations of the institutions of the dominant culture, the Chinese were not slaves on par with Blacks. They were immigrants. But to support the objectification of the Chinese as slaves, images that were used in connection with Blacks were applied to them. References to the "Middle Passage" were invoked in the voyages of the Chinese to the United States, but the passages were not similar. Additionally, there was no period of seasoning where the Chinese were broken in as slaves as there was for Blacks. Although many laws attempted to equate the Chinese with Blacks, there were differences. The Chinese could marry, they had control of their children, they were permitted to learn to read and write, they could practice their culture, they could change jobs, and they had freedom of movement. In short, the Chinese had a measure of control over their lives that was not allowed African slaves.

The decade from 1880 to 1890 was crucial for people of color in the United States. Jim Crow laws were initiated against African-Americans in Tennessee in 1881, the Chinese Exclusion Act was signed into law in 1882, in 1883 the Civil Rights Act of 1875 was declared unconstitutional, and the last major battle with Native Americans occurred at Wounded Knee in 1890. By 1885 Africa had been sliced up by major European powers, an opportunity in which the United States had not participated. By effectively curbing its ethnics of color, the United States had successfully established "internal colonies" in preparation for its imperialist ventures with dark-skinned people in the following decades: Hawaii, the Philippines, Puerto Rico, and Guam in 1898, Samoa in 1899, and the Panama Canal Zone in 1903.

The dominant culture had clear reasons for attempting to blacken the images of the Chinese: to prepare for imperialistic adventures and the consolidation of all people of color into one broad, easily managed, conventional image. African-American women writers have recognized the attempt to distort their history and images and have tried to rectify the distortions in their writings. With one exception, Sui Sin Far, Chinese-American women writers have not acknowledged the existence of this history and thus have not incorporated it into their writing. They have instead adopted a distant, exotic China or a mythicized Chinatown as the focus of their writing.

NOTES

1. Stuart Creighton Miller, *The Unwelcome Immigrant. The American Image of the Chinese, 1785–1882* (Berkeley: University of California Press, 1974), 173.

2. Gunter Barth, *Bitter Strength. A History of the Chinese in the United States, 1850–1870* (Cambridge: Harvard University Press, 1964), 189.

3. In use since 1638. Originally of Tamil origin, meaning "to hire" or "hireling," an unskilled, cheaply employed laborer in or from Asia, especially India and China.

4. Carey McWilliams, *Brothers under the Skin* (Boston: Little, Brown and Company, 1943), 85.

5. Barth, 195.

6. Ibid., 196. Shih-Shan Henry Tsai, "The Chinese in Arkansas," *Amerasia Journal* (Spring/Summer 1981): 6.

7. In Louisiana the racial classification was different. "In the absence of a separate color category for the Chinese before the census of 1870, the group was

classified as white. . . . In the 1870 census, enumerators were instructed to use the separate category Chinese for all persons of that ancestry." Lucy M. Cohen, *Chinese in the Post–Civil War South. A People without a History* (Baton Rouge: Louisiana State University Press, 1984), 167.

8. James W. Loewen, *The Mississippi Chinese. Between Black and White* (Prospect Heights, IL: Waveland Press, Inc., 1971, 1988), 1.

9. The Page Law, 1878, effectively limited the immigration of Chinese women. "California banned marriages between whites and Chinese in 1906. Similar laws were passed in Arizona, Georgia, Idaho, Louisiana, Mississippi, Missouri, Nebraska, Nevada, South Dakota, Utah, Virginia and Wyoming. California repealed its law in 1948, and the Supreme Court in 1967 ruled the other miscegenation laws unconstitutional." Jack Chen, *The Chinese of America* (New York: Harper and Row, 1980), 154. See also Pauli Murray, ed., *State Laws on Race and Color* (Cincinnati: Women's Division of Christian Service Board of Missions and Church Extension, Methodist Church, 1950).

10. Loewen, 136.

11. Ibid.

12. Robert Seto Quan and Julian B. Roebuck, *Lotus among the Magnolias: The Mississippi Chinese* (Jackson: University of Mississippi Press, 1971), 48.

13. Ibid., 45.

14. Loewen, 67.

15. Ibid.

16. See Loewen, chapter 4.

17. Ibid., 5, 76, 79.

18. Ibid., 86.

19. Ibid., 82.

20. Ibid., 96.

21. Ibid., 79.

22. Rose Hum Lee, *The Chinese in the United States of America* (Hong Kong: Hong Kong University Press, 1960), 370; Cheng-Tsu Wu, *"Chink!" A Documentary History of Anti-Chinese Prejudice in America* (New York: World Publishing, 1972), 223; Chen, 131; Loewen, 135; Victor G. Nee and Brett de Bary Nee, *Longtime Californ': A Documentary Study of an American Chinatown* (Stanford, CA: Stanford University Press, 1972), 385.

23. A member of a people of southern Africa.

24. Miller, 44.

25. M. J. A. Roorda Smit also examined the similarities between Chinese and Hottentots in "Contributions to the Knowledge of the Hottentot Race," *Popular Science Review* (May 1881): 147–159. Smit writes "I have seen a Chinese and a Hottentot both serving in the same hotel; as they were dressed almost in the same style, we were constantly confounding them, taking the Asiatic for the African, and *vice versa*." He also claims that "the affinities of the Hottentot language [are] rather connected . . . with the languages of High Asia."

26. Ronald Takaki, *Strangers from a Different Shore. A History of Asian Americans* (New York: Penguin Books, 1989), 100; Terry E. Boswell, "A Split

Labor Market Analysis of Discrimination Against Chinese Immigrants, 1850–1882," *American Sociological Review* 51 (June 1986): 358.

27. Miller, 151.

28. Ibid., 153.

29. Ibid.

30. Nee and Nee, 57n5.

31. Elmer Clarence Sandmeyer, *The Anti-Chinese Move in California* (Urbana: University of Illinois Press, 1973, 1991), 26.

32. Boswell, 357, and Sandmeyer, 25.

33. Marshall De Motte, "California—White or Yellow?" *The Annals of the American Academy* (January 1921): 18.

34. Dan Caldwell, "The Negroization of the Chinese Stereotype in California," *The Historical Society of Southern California* 53 (1971): 128.

35. Takaki, 102.

36. Caldwell, 128.

37. Takaki, 101.

38. Caldwell, 131.

39. Lerone Bennet, *Before the Mayflower. A History of the Negro in America, 1619–1964* (Baltimore: Penguin Books, 1968, 1962), 222.

40. Chen, 185.

41. "Chinese White Marriages in New York," *Harpers Weekly* (October 3, 1857): 630.

42. Maxine Hong Kingston, *China Men* (New York: Ballantine Books, 1980), 153.

43. Denis Kearney was an Irish-American, anti-Chinese agitator who vehemently attacked Chinese immigrants for working for starvation wages and robbing Euro-American workers of jobs.

44. Wu, 153.

45. C. F. Holder, "Chinese Slavery in America," *North American Review* 165 (September 1897): 290, 292.

46. Kenneth M. Stampp, *The Peculiar Institution: Slavery in the Ante-bellum South* (New York: Vintage Books, 1956), 260–61.

47. Paula Giddings, *When and Where I Enter. The Impact of Black Women on Race and Sex in America* (New York: Bantam Books, 1984), 35.

48. Ibid., 31.

49. Gerald Stanley, "Frank Pixley and the Heathen Chinese," *Phylon* (September 1979): 227.

50. Congressional Record, 43rd Congress, 2nd session, Dec. 7, 1874, 3–4.

51. Sandmeyer, 81.

52. Takaki, 40.

53. Ibid., 121.

54. A. J. Brown, "Lo Mo of San Francisco; Donaldina Cameron and Her Work for the Rescue of Chinese Girls," *Missionary Review of the World* 55 (May 1932): 263–66; "Chinese Slavery," *Westminster Review* 165 (April 1906): 458–62; "Chinese Slavery Condemned," *Westminster Review* 165 (April 1906):

217–20; M. Lake, "Chinese Slave Girls in America," *Missionary Review of the World* 26 (July 1903): 532–33; E. V. Robbins, "Chinese Slave Girls," *Overland* 51 (January 1903): 100–103; C. R. Shepherd, "Chinese Girl Slavery in America," *Missionary Review of the World* 46 (November 1923): 893–98.

55. "The Chinese in California," *Lippincotts Magazine* (July 1868): 41.

56. *New York Times*, February 25, 1869, 4–7, 5–2; "The Chinese Habeas Corpus Cases in San Francisco," *New York Times*, March 2, 1869, 1–6; "Chinese Women," *New York Times*, March 17, 1869, 11; *New York Times*, July 30, 1869, 8–1.

57. Nee and Nee, 21.

58. Chen, 151.

59. Sandmeyer, 48.

60. Miller, 185.

61. *New York Times*, June 11, 1883, 1.

62. Russell T. Herrick, "The Police Run Wild in Cleveland," *The Nation* (October 14, 1925): 401.

63. Frank Norris, *The Third Circle* (New York: John Lane, 1909).

64. Miller, 185.

65. Ibid.

66. "Yick Wo," *The Nation* (June 6, 1895): 438–39.

67. Ibid.

68. Chen, 228.

69. Frank Chin, "Confessions of the Chinatown Cowboy," *Bulletin of Concerned Asian Scholars* 4 (Fall 1972): 60.

70. Takaki, 246.

71. Peter Kwong, *The New Chinatown* (New York: Hall and Wang, 1987), 14.

72. Ivan Light, "From Vice District to Tourist Attraction: The Moral Career of American Chinatowns, 1880–1940," *Pacific Historical Review* (1974): 391.

73. Takaki, 93.

74. Miller, 185.

75. In addition to the fact that both groups are visible minorities, the dominant society has assigned other stereotypical traits to Blacks and Chinese; for example, they all look alike, and they are filthy, licentious, and fecund.

Chapter Two

Mammies, Mulattas, Sluts, and Sapphires

Representations of the African-American slave woman as breeder and sexual object, as farm worker, or domestic and industrial laborer do not seem to exist in the early literature of the United States. No literary portraits, either authentic or distorted, were drawn of African-American women for almost two centuries after their arrival in Jamestown, Virginia.

In Virginia, the 1624–1625 census showed the presence of twenty-three Africans: eleven males, ten females, and two children. This group of Africans was probably the last to enter and work in the United States as indentured servants. Within a short time, their status and their lives would be restricted by ever more stringent and repressive legislation, which, while constricting African-American men, even further constrained African-American women.

Before long, several state legislatures had adopted the principle of *partus sequitur ventrem*, that is, the child inherits the condition of the mother. With this ruling, the African female in the American colonies acquired a new status. Planters recognized that they could more quickly amass necessary capital by breeding the African slave women. As a result, enforced breeding of Africans became the norm.

The African woman did not freely accept another's control of her body just as she did not freely accept slavery; she had to be prepared for it, and this preparation began in Africa. The African economy during the seventeenth century was based on agriculture, which in some areas nearly approached the complexity of the plantation system in the Southern states. The traditional African agricultural and social systems required that women perform most of the strenuous agricultural labor. bell hooks comments that "white male observers of African culture in the 18th and 19th century were astounded and impressed by the African male's subjugation of the African female."[1] It was not long before it occurred to the slave traders that the African female, accustomed as she was to the arduous physical labor of the African agricultural community, would also be useful on the plantation. Therefore, her preparation for the Southern cotton fields began in Africa. This preparation for chattel slavery was continued on the slave ship. While aboard ship, the African female was kept in a state of perpetual undress as a constant reminder of her sexual availability.

If the shipboard experience had not sufficiently humbled the African female, then further indignities awaited her in order that her behavior conform to the slave owner's perception of appropriate slave behavior. The African female slave was paraded nude on the slave block and inspected by the Euro-American slave buyers. As Dorothy Sterling observes, "At a time when white women were thought immodest if they so much as showed their feet, slave girls, scantily clad at best, were required to strip for inspection by would be purchasers."[2] Next came the removal of name and status, the dispersion of groups so that no common language could exist, and the removal of any overt sign of African heritage. African females were more brutalized and terrorized than males not only because of their gender but also because they would be working in Euro-American households, and for this work they apparently needed more "seasoning." (This is the process whereby an African is "broken" and changed into a slave. S/He is brutalized into "acceptable" behavior.)[3]

Contrary to popular belief, the male slave was allowed to maintain some vestiges of the traditional masculine role. Both Angela Davis and bell hooks argue that history does not record that slave men were forced to perform tasks considered feminine. Slave women were exploited as laborers in both the fields and in industry.

Not only were the slave women industrial and farm laborers, jobs labeled unsuitable for Euro-American women; they were workers in domestic households and also became breeders and sexual objects for Euro-American males. Much of the history of the sexual exploitation of slave women has been ignored. Historians and researchers have instead considered these sexual acts miscegenation or seduction on the part of the slave woman rather than a form of rape.

None of the circumstances of the African-American woman as slave is present in most eighteenth-century and nineteenth-century historical accounts. Nor were statistics on breeding, forced concubinage, and industrial and field labor recorded in Euro-American writing. During the colonial

period, the new Euro-Americans were more interested in their own physical and religious survival than in the Africans among them—other than
to maintain the Africans' enslavement with increasingly repressive laws.
Accordingly, colonial literature did feature some African-American characters, but the Africans were nebulous background figures who were not
essential to the story. Although fictional representations of African women
were absent from colonial literature, some representations were present in
political writing of the period. Thomas Jefferson wrote in Query XIV of
Notes on the State of Virginia that the orangutan has preference for the
Black woman over that of his own species. Jefferson promulgated this
conception of African women at the time that he had allegedly established
a sexual relationship with one of his slave women, Sally Hemmings.
Echoing Jefferson, John Randolph, the Virginia statesman, expressed
doubts that Africans could be emancipated because "their women would
be debased without measure if set free."4 No doubt the exploitation would
occur because of the looseness of the morals of slave women.

It was not until the early nineteenth century that African-American
characters began to appear in fiction with frequency. Authors such as
Washington Irving, *Salmagundi* (1807) and *The Knickerbocker History of
New York* (1809); James Fenimore Cooper, *The Spy* (1821) and *The Last
of the Mohicans* (1826); and Herman Melville, *Moby Dick* (1851) and
Benito Cereno (1855) began to incorporate African-Americans into their
writings. Although the characters were primarily male, a female stereotype
was emerging.

This newly emerging stereotype of the African-American female deviated significantly from that of the Euro-American female norm, which
frequently also was stereotyped, but in a flattering manner. These stereotypes amply demonstrate the generalizations that have been used to justify
racism. The African-American female characters that have appeared in
American fiction can be divided into four categories. One is the tragic
mulatta, usually the offspring of a Euro-American slave-owner and a slave
woman. (Although *mulatto* is the common term used to describe a person
of African and European ancestry, it is masculine. The feminine form,
mulatta, will be used here.) Another is the loose woman, or what Nancy
Tischler prefers to designate as "the black siren." She is "sexually amoral,
sprinkling the world liberally with yard children."5 The Aunt Jemima
image is the turbaned, good-humored, obese African-American female
who cares for the children of Euro-Americans. She is passive, compas-
sionate, long-suffering, and submissive. This "mammy" image usually can
be seen in opposition to the Sapphire, "a domineering type who rules the
family, her husband included. She is seen as a masculinized female who

must be subordinated in order that the Black male may take his rightful place in society."[6] These four images of African-American women tend to be the most prevalent in American fiction. Race and gender will eventually collide with fiction to support negative, long-lasting stereotypes of African-American women.

According to *The Oxford English Dictionary*, *mulatta* is derived from the Spanish or Portuguese word meaning "young mule," hence one of mixed race or one who is the offspring of a European and an African. In continuing the mule imagery, the mulatta is also a bearer of burdens, and some nineteenth-century racial zealots theorized that, like the mule, the mulatta was also sterile.[7] The earliest known usage of *mulatto* is 1622; however, it appears that the characters usually described in late nineteenth-century or early twentieth-century American fiction as mulatta are in actuality quadroons or octoroons, a person who is one-eighth African. By the early nineteenth century, depictions of the offspring of the illicit relationship between the slave-owner and the slave woman had evolved into the stereotype of the tragic mulatta.

The appearance of the mulatta character in the early nineteenth century may be attributed to many factors. Judith Berzon speculates that one reason may have been ignorance, and another might have been that in order to dramatize the horrors of slavery, white abolitionists would present heroes and heroines who were quasi-white.[8]

These mulatta characters all seemed similar; they were so much the same that eventually they developed into archetypes.[9] The fictional mulatta (Clotelle, Camille in J. T. Trowbridge's *Neighbor Jackwood*, 1857, or Cassy in *Archy Moore*, 1856) was usually the child of a Southern slave-owner and one of his favorite slave women. From the father, the mulatta inherited superior mental abilities, physical beauty, independence, and individuality, and from the mother, "savage primitivism." Despite her beauty and intellectual abilities, the mulatta was still a slave, and having to cope with the reality of slavery caused suffering, hostility, and alienation. Nevertheless, the independent, individualistic spirit of the father would surface, and the mulatta would rebel in different ways. For example, she is insubordinate and attempts to escape to the North. If the escape to freedom was successful, then the mulatta became a happy, prosperous, and reputable citizen in an African-American community. If the revolt or attempted escape failed, death was met honorably and defiantly. Nonetheless, she remains tragic; the inability to be one or the other, European or African, is the tragedy of the mulatta.

One of the earliest characterizations of the tragic mulatta (or in this case, probably an octoroon) is Cora Munro in James Fenimore Cooper's *The*

Last of the Mohicans (1826). Cora is not a slave; she is a legitimate child who lives in freedom with her Euro-American father and half-sister Alice. Although Cora is beautiful, intelligent, and strong, she is rejected by Major Heyward because of her racial background, although he refuses to admit it. He clearly prefers the spotless, racially "pure" Alice. Alice is contrasted with Cora, the dark-haired passionate woman, who is the child of this British officer and a "lady whose misfortune it was . . . to be descended, remotely, from that unfortunate class who are so basely enslaved to administer to the wants of a luxurious people."[10] Alice, on the other hand, is blond, sexless, weak, and empty-headed.

Of the two sisters, Cora is a more likeable character. She is depicted as dark, strong, dignified, controlled, and respectful of the Native Americans who accompany their group. Alice is shallow, dependent, and ultra-feminine; she faints on cue. With her unfortunate trace of African ancestry, Cora comes to a tragic end (as mulattas must) with the knife of one of the Huron warriors in her chest. In his creation of the mulatta, Cooper sets the tone for the way the mulatta character is rendered throughout the years in American literature. Nevertheless, Cora is a rare deviation from this stereotype; she is legitimate, publicly acknowledged, and accepted by her father.

Several years after the publication of *The Last of the Mohicans*, a group of Abolitionist writers began to publish anti-slavery novels, which they hoped would influence the American public to turn against the institution of slavery. Many of the characters developed by these Abolitionist writers became stereotypes in American fiction. Among this early group of Abolitionist writers were Harriet Beecher Stowe (*Uncle Tom's Cabin*, 1852), W. W. Smith (*The Yankee Slave Driver*, 1860), William Wells Brown (*Clotelle*, 1867), J. T. Trowbridge (*Neighbor Jackwood*, 1857), and Richard Hildreth.

Richard Hildreth, a historian, supposedly produced the first anti-slavery novel, *Archy Moore, The White Slave or Memoirs of a Fugitive*. The novel was first published anonymously in 1836. In 1856, twenty-five years after Nat Turner's revolt, Hildreth admitted authorship and enlarged and republished his novel as *The White Slave*. Although the main character is a male, the novel will be dealt with briefly here because it develops the stereotyping of "the white slave, the rebel slave, the octoroon girl, the unfeeling Yankee overseer, and the lustful planter,"[11] who will reappear in later American fiction.

Archy Moore, who is the son of Colonel Moore and one of his slave women, never adjusted well to slavery. He seemed to believe that although he was a slave, his Euro-American appearance and the color of his skin should have exempted him from slavery.[12] Archy Moore felt that he was of a higher caste than the darker slaves. To a certain extent, this caste system was reinforced by the slave-owning class. This colorism on the part of the mulatto not only has persisted in literature but has been reflected in society.[13]

For publicly acknowledging his relationship to Colonel Moore and "marrying" Cassy, whom Colonel Moore has chosen as his next mistress even though she is his child, Archy is sold. He is bought and sold several times before he finally escapes to freedom.

After escaping slavery, Archy Moore makes his way to Boston, where he ships out as a deckhand on a ship bound for England. During the voyage, the ship is attacked by privateers, and Archy chooses to join the attackers. Eventually, Archy is given command of his own ship. His share of the booty makes him a wealthy man. After amassing a fortune, Archy returns to the United States to search for Cassy and their missing child.

Cassy as a character is not as clearly drawn as Archy (although this is as it should be, since Archy is the protagonist of the novel). Cassy, although darker than Archie, is also the child of Colonel Moore and one of his slave mistresses. She is beautiful, graceful, and elegant, equal to the patrician beauties of Virginia. Cassy's "marriage" to Archy is the cause of his being sold away from Colonel Moore's plantation. After Archy's departure, Colonel Moore's pursuit of Cassy becomes more persistent.[14] Through the use of various feminine tactics, she manages to ward off his advances until she decides that she must escape. She leaves the plantation and has a series of adventures similar to Archy's until they are finally reunited at a slave auction, where Archy plays a major role in their emancipation.

Archy Moore presents characters and situations that were to become important aspects of the American fiction that dealt with the African-American. Among these situations are those that make use of the mulatta slave. Because Richard Hildreth did not fully develop these women, it was left to later writers to develop fully the character of the tragic mulatta. Nevertheless, in his conception of Cassy, Hildreth seemingly followed the model of Cora Munro as portrayed by James Fenimore Cooper.

One of the earliest examples of the use of the tragic mulatta as protagonist is in *Clotelle* (1867) by the ex-slave and anti-slavery agent, William Wells Brown. The book is based on the actual escape of Ellen Craft. Clotelle, the protagonist, is more fortunate than her mother or her aunt. Clotelle's mother commits suicide, and her aunt is returned to slavery after the death of the aunt's husband, a Vermont doctor. Clotelle is sold from one place to another until she finally becomes the slave of a very kind woman. While in this home, Clotelle falls in love with a handsome, dark-skinned slave, Jerome. She helps Jerome escape execution disguised as a woman after he physically resists a Euro-American man. Clotelle takes Jerome's place, remaining undetected in his jail cell. (She is an octoroon, almost white, and he is black.) For this act of defiance she is severely beaten, sold, and sent to New Orleans. There, Antoine Devenant, a British military officer, falls in love with her after first seeing her in the slave market. "The unequalled beauty of Clotelle had dazzled his eyes, and every look that she gave was a dagger that went to his heart."[15] Again, the color of her skin places her above the common slave, and Devenant deplores that she was bought.

Devenant eventually helps Clotelle to escape to Europe where they marry. The newly married couple then leave for India, where Devenant joins his military unit. Soon after their arrival in India, he is killed in battle with the natives. Clotelle returns to Europe with her only child and becomes a member of the Devenant family. There, she is finally reunited with her father and with her former lover, Jerome. She and Jerome marry, and the father is convinced to return to the United States in order to free his slaves.

Clotelle is important in the history of American fiction for several reasons. For a considerable period it was thought to be the first African-American novel, it dramatizes the evils of slavery through the sexual victimization of a beautiful "white" (octoroon) slave woman, and it supposedly presents slavery's evils from an African-American point of view. But Clotelle does not differ significantly from fictional mulattas created by Euro-American writers. She is defiant, independent, ambitious, beautiful, and intelligent, which were characteristic of popular novels of the time. However, unlike mulattas created by previous writers, Clotelle does not seem to possess racially specific attributes. Clotelle is intelligent and ambitious. These qualities, along with her longing for freedom, are not peculiar to Euro-Americans but because she recognizes the injustice of one person's owning another.

Following Emancipation, Reconstruction caused another conflict between the African-American's attempt to assume his or her legal rights and the Euro-American's determination to continue his monopoly of privileges. Again, there was an opportunity for the writer/activist to take up the pen. This time, however, there were two groups of such writers, one representing each side of the issue. The pro-slavery writer had not previously used the mulatta because of a refusal to admit the existence of miscegenation. But the Southerner now insisted upon the protection of his privileges from the infringement of the newly freed African-American.

Sterling Brown suggests that this idealization of slavery was necessary to justify the institution as a system of protection for the Africans.[16]

Among those writers who idealized slavery but at the same time depicted the mulatto as a dangerous, inhuman element among the freedmen were Thomas Nelson Page (*In Ole Virginia*, 1887) and the Reverend Thomas Dixon (*The Leopard's Spots*, 1902, and *The Clansman*, 1905). Their provocative caricatures painted the mulatto male as a brutal rapist of Euro-American women, a corrupter of Euro-American men, and a usurper of political power.

In *The Leopard's Spots* and *The Clansman*, Dixon presents three significant biracial characters: George Harris, a Harvard graduate who wishes to woo a Euro-American woman; Lydia Brown, the housekeeper and mistress of Radical Reconstructionist Senator Stoneman, whose insidious influence over the senator imperils the United States; and Silas Lynch, Lydia's mulatto lover. Lynch, who has the "head of Caesar and the eyes of the jungle," harbors intense political ambitions. With white power and a "white mind" in a black body, Lynch demonstrates, according to Juanita Stark, the dual nature of and cultural attitudes toward the mulatto, which is one of the clearest in literature.[17]

Thomas Dixon and Thomas Nelson Page placed their political propaganda that disparaged African-Americans in a contemporary setting. George Washington Cable, a liberal on racial policies, had a more sympathetic perspective and looked backward at the past. In two major works (*Old Creole Days*, 1879, and *The Grandissimes*, 1880), Cable has been praised by Sterling Brown for his just and sympathetic treatment of the African-American. Cable wrote fiction set in New Orleans that sometimes dealt with the mulatta, his use of which helped establish the tragic mulatta as a stereotype. As Sterling Brown has pointed out, Cable's portraits of the mulatta are drawn from a specific situation in the past that was more common in New Orleans than in other parts of the South. Brown is specifically referring to the quadroon balls, which were little more than romanticized slave markets, where Euro-American men were able to purchase near-white slave mistresses. Although Brown considers Cable one of the finest creators of African-American characters in the nineteenth century, William S. Braithwaite believes that Cable "did little more than idealize the aristocratic tradition of the Old South with the Negro as literary foil."[18]

Moving from the South of Dixon, Page, and Cable to the urban North, one sees that William Dean Howells, novelist, critic, and editor, used the theme of the tragic mulatta in a different manner. In *An Imperative Duty* (1892), Rhoda Aldgate is the legitimate daughter of a Euro-American male and a Louisiana creole[19] mother. After the death of her parents, Rhoda, with her inky black hair and eyes and olive complexion, is brought up as a Euro-American child by her father's sister and her brother-in-law, Mr. and Mrs. Meredith. The aunt, Caroline Meredith, knows the truth about Rhoda and is wary of the threat of atavism.[20] Dr. Olney, a friend of the family, tries to relieve Mrs. Meredith's anxiety by reassuring her that the chances of reversion to a black ancestor are remote.

However, Mrs. Meredith decides that Rhoda must be told the truth of her ancestry. Rhoda reacts hysterically to this knowledge, although she has always pretended to have a nonbiased attitude toward African-Americans. Before she was aware that she was Black, Rhoda had found the African-American waiters in the hotel charming, gentle, and gracious. But after learning her true identity, Rhoda's attitude toward African-Americans takes on a more racist tone. She begins to imagine them as pets. Instead of finding the African-Americans charming, gentle, and gracious, they become "hideous by the standards of all His creatures."[21]

Trying to accept the fact that she is one-sixteenth African, she flees to the African-American community to "find" herself. But again she is repelled by their "sad repulsive visages of a frog-like ugliness . . . they were all abhorrent."[22]

Subsequently Rhoda is convinced that she is one-sixteenth African and decides that if she can learn to accept and love African-Americans, then she can accept herself. With feelings of superiority, she decides that perhaps she should go to New Orleans (the home of her mother) in order to assist in the "elevation" of African-Americans. However, Dr. Olney, to whom Mrs. Meredith had entrusted the truth about Rhoda's ancestry, finally persuades her to accept his marriage proposal. They marry and go to live in Italy but not happily ever after.

As a Euro-American woman, Rhoda is self-centered, self-confident, and self-assured, but as an African-American woman she changes. After acknowledging her "Blackness," Rhoda's self-esteem is significantly lowered; she becomes frenzied. Her "Africanness" seemingly makes her distinct, peculiar. She becomes the antithesis of the Bloomingdale sisters, who are serene, still and blond. However, after moving to Italy where her coloring will not be suspect, Olney observes that "the sunny-natured antetypes of her mother's race had not endowed her with more of the heaven-born cheerfulness with which it meets contumely and injustice."[23] Ironically, Howells, one of the founders of the National Association for the Advancement of Colored People, ends his novella by stating the racist theories of his times.

Duty and masks override the theme of the tragic mulatta. Mrs.
Meredith's duty is to inform Rhoda of her slight African heritage. Her duty
cannot be evaded or avoided. To do so would mean that Rhoda would bear
Black children. Rhoda's duty is to accept this heritage and the injustice
and social inferiority that accompany it. All the characters wear masks,
pretending to be that which they are not. Mrs. Meredith pretends to be
unbiased and accepting of all groups, although she commits suicide after
informing Rhoda of her heritage. Dr. Olney also wears the mask of
pretense. He pretends to be free of racial prejudice, although he unwittingly assigns Rhoda racially specific attributes and is unhappy when those
attributes are not in her personality. Rhoda wears the densest mask of them
all. Learning her true identity should not necessarily signal a change in
personality or convictions.

Howell's late nineteenth-century sympathetic characterization of the
tragic mulatta did not signal the disappearance of the character in American fiction. Major American writers continued the use of the character.
Writers as varied as Gertrude Stein, *Melanctha: Each One as She May*
(1909); Fannie Hurst, *Imitation of Life* (1933); William Faulkner,
Absalom! Absalom! (1936), *Go Down Moses* (1940), and *Light in August*
(1948); Sinclair Lewis, *Kingsblood Royal* (1948); and Robert Penn War-
ren, *Band of Angels* (1955), all used the mulatta character in their writings.
The use of the character was not limited to Euro-American writers. Not
only did William Wells Brown make fictional use of the tragic mulatta in
Clotelle, but so did other African-American male writers. Charles
Chestnutt, *The House Behind the Cedars* (1900); Rudolph Fisher, *The
Walls of Jericho* (1928); Langston Hughes, *The Mulatto* (1931), and *The
Ways of White Folks* (1933); Ralph Ellison, *Invisible Man* (1952); and
many others prominently featured mulatta characters. Frequently these
novels by African-American male writers dealt with the problem of
"passing," which was among the myriad problems facing the mulatta.

The mulatta was also frequently portrayed as "loose" in American
fiction. The use of the African-American woman as breeder, the refusal to
allow legal marriages between slaves, and the different physical appearance between African and European-American women all served to label
the African-American during and after slavery as a loose woman. In more
recent times, the ready availability of the African-American female during
slavery was widely reported. J. C. Furnas writes,

The slave woman was to be had for the taking. Boys on and about the plantation
inevitably learned to use her, and having acquired a habit, often continued it into
manhood and even after marriage. . . . Efforts to build up a taboo against

miscegenation made little progress. I do not mean to imply . . . that it was universal. . . . Many men in the South . . . rigidly abstained from such liaisons and scorned those who indulged. Nevertheless, that they were sufficiently common is unquestionable.[24]

The sexual use of slave women led to the accepted belief that they were inherently immoral, and thus exploitable. Gerda Lerner believes that even after Emancipation, the sexual exploitation of African-American women continued. But to support the race theories of the time, new myths of African-Americans had to be created. One of these was the myth of the "bad" black woman. During slavery the belief that there were different levels of sexuality between African-Americans and Euro-Americans evolved. African-American men were believed to have greater sexual potency than Euro-American men; therefore, its was reasoned, the African-American woman also had to be more licentious than the Euro-American woman. If African-American women were more wanton, then they deserved none of the respect given to Euro-American women. Thus, the African-American woman could be sexually assaulted with impunity. All African-American women, with no exceptions, were sluts "according to racist mythology . . . To assault her and exploit her sexually was not reprehensible and carried with it none of the normal communal sanctions against such behavior."[25]

Consequently, Lerner continues, "the myth of the black rapist of white women is the twin of the myth of the bad black woman—both designed to apologize for and facilitate the continued exploitation of black men and women."[26] Thus, one of the predominant images of the African-American woman in American society became that of the "fallen woman, the whore, the slut, the prostitute."[27]

Some African-American men began to point out the discrepancy between words and actions. Walter White, an outstanding anti-lynching leader and Executive Secretary of the NAACP, wrote in *The Rope and the Faggot: A Biography of Judge Lynch* (1929) of the sanctimonious and hypocritical words and deeds of a Euro-American office holder who decried the state of immorality existing among African-American women while at the same time "possessed a considerable family by a Negro mistress as well as one by his white wife."[28]

Thirty-six years after White wrote the preceding indictment, Calvin Hernton, an African-American writer, espoused these earlier sexist-racist theories in *Sex and Racism in America* (1965) where he states that the "Negro woman became promiscuous and loose . . . [and could be had] for the taking . . . [because] . . . she had no other morality by which to shape her womanhood.[29] And Mel Watkins and Jay David interpret African-American women on the dust cover of *To Be a Black Woman. Portraits in Fact and Fiction* (1970) as "the sexual myth incarnate—a plaything, an illicit pleasure for the white man . . . she accepted the myth and often adopted a life style that actualized it."[30] These African-American male writers readily accepted the Euro-American-created myth of the African-American woman without having analyzed it.

This characterization of the loose African-American female as immoral is the opposite of the more moral Euro-American female, who was linked, by contrast, with the Euro-American "cult of true womanhood" in the early 1830s. The cult numbered among its basic tenets domesticity, submissiveness, piety, and purity. African-American women now had to acquire Euro-American middle-class values and, as Paula Giddings indicates, to "overcome notions about the relationship of class—as well as color—to morality."[31]

African-American women were lacking the essential qualities of "ladyhood," which included not only domesticity and chastity but also leisure because most African-American woman worked outside the home. All of this combined to make her a woman but not a lady. Therefore, the African-American woman became a very vulnerable subhuman species of female. Added to the above-mentioned characteristics that maligned her character were state and local laws that derived from the Slave Code, one of which stated, "Rape committed on a female slave is an offense not recognized by law."[32] This attitude formulated during slavery seems to have transcended time and entered American fiction.

African-American female characters consonant with the pattern of loose women were created by Du Bose Heywood in *Porgy* (1925) and Dorothy and Du Bose Heywood in the play *Mamba's Daughters* (1939). Heywood (1885–1940), a South Carolina–born novelist, poet, and dramatist, is probably best known for the folk-opera *Porgy and Bess*. Heywood wrote the libretto, and he collaborated with Ira Gershwin on the lyrics. George Gershwin composed the music. In the novella *Porgy*, Bess, the principal female character, lives in Charleston, South Carolina, and is "completely primitive,"[33] a drunken, scar-faced, cocaine-abusing woman who dresses "gorgeously in the clashing crimsons and purples that [she] loved."[34] She is a proud, aloof woman whose behavior causes her to be alienated from the more decent women of Catfish Row. She is completely amoral. After moving in with Porgy uninvited and without "benefit of clergy," she regained her old bearing, which "had so infuriated the virtuous during her evil days, . . . and in her bettered condition forced a resentful respect from her feminine traducers."[35] She is transformed by her relationship with

Porgy, but she is weak. Bess tries to leave her old life behind her but is constantly thwarted by men with long memories and little tolerance for reformed women. While on a picnic, Bess goes into the woods to pick palmetto leaves. She accidentally meets Crown, a former lover, to whom she responds passionately. Finally, she is unable to continue the fight against her previous life, and she returns to degradation in the North. Bess loses the battle for propriety not because she is weak or because Euro-American society has undermined her but because she is a Black woman. She is defined by her race and gender.

In contrast, Mamba, Hagar, and Lissa are three generations of women who continue to fight for a better life. In *Mamba's Daughters*, Mamba, the grandmother, is a strong, intelligent, and ambitious although uneducated woman who seizes the chance to improve the life of her granddaughter, Lissa. Mamba, like most of the other women in the play, has never been married and does not feel ashamed of her unmarried state. She has one child, Hagar.

Hagar is a hard-working, foolhardy, "simple-minded" Amazon. She "can chop as much cotton now as any of de mens."[36] She puts this strength to good use by supporting her mother and her daughter, Lissa. She is a good mother to Lissa, always putting Lissa's concerns first. Yet when Hagar is sent to the Sea Islands to work off the probation she has received for fighting with a man and taking money he owed her for laundry, Lissa does not want to visit her.

Above all, Hagar is a good mother and understands Lissa's reluctance to visit her. Tischler explains that being a good mother is a part of the "fallen woman" syndrome. "She provides for the child by handing him or her over to a more reliable grandparent and continues on her own path of sexual abandon."[37] Hagar does not completely fit this image; after Lissa's birth, Hagar does not continue her old life-style of sexual abandon, instead becoming celibate. Although prior to Lissa's birth there had been many men, afterward it becomes a point of honor with Hagar that not only has she been sexually incorruptible, "But neber any white man." [38]

Hagar also realizes that she cannot become a part of the life that Mamba has created for Lissa because she is not "good" enough. Hagar seems to sum up the bifurcated vision that Euro-American writers have of African-American women: African-American women may be sluts, but, as Tischler has pointed out, they are also good mothers.

Lissa, who has become socially superior to both Hagar and Mamba, is ashamed of both. Lissa has assumed Euro-American values and sees Hagar through these values as an ignorant, foul-smelling peasant. When Lissa finally goes to the Sea Islands to visit Hagar, she is "scrupulously polite,

undoubtedly she feels superior to her surroundings."[39] Lissa is also
ashamed that the women of her family have not been legally married. After
Hagar has gone to her rescue when she is raped by Gilly Bluton, Lissa
hysterically explains that she cannot become pregnant and give birth to an
illegitimate child as Mamba and Hagar have. She is different; she has a
different set of values.

But Lissa does become pregnant and delivers a child, who dies an hour
after birth. Gilly Bluton, suspecting that the child has been murdered,
begins to blackmail Hagar and Mamba. Lissa, in the meantime, has
become a very successful singer in New York, and Mamba and Hagar do
not want her embarrassed by Gilly Bluton's revelation. To stop the
blackmail, Hagar kills Gilly and then commits suicide.

These three women are not bad women; they are simply not Euro-American women. Mamba, Hagar, and Lissa deviate from Euro-American
cultural patterns. They have their own set of values, which are at variance
to those of the majority group. Mamba and her family are judged by a set
of standards that implicitly state that a single-parent household is deviant.
Since single-parent family units are usually female-headed, they are
economically insecure. Because the dominant society sets the rules, these
women's actions can be misinterpreted. Circumstances cause those qualities that are positive in them—strong kinship bonds, strong work orientations, adaptability of family roles, strong religious orientations[40]—but
that are seen by the dominant Euro-American society as negative.

Another view of these "negative" qualities of African-American women
is found in Paul Green's *White Dresses*. Green won the Pulitzer Prize in
1927 for his play *In Abraham's Bosom*, which also dealt with African-
Americans.

In *White Dresses*, Green creates a different version of the African-American slut. Set in rural North Carolina at the turn of the century, the play
portrays Mary McLean as in love with a Euro-American male, Hugh
Morgan, and her love apparently is reciprocated. But Henry Morgan,
Hugh's father, tells Mary that he has sent Hugh away. Morgan warns Mary
that she must marry the African-American male, Jim, whom he has chosen
for her, or she and her aged grandmother must leave the farm. Mary refuses
to marry Jim because, like Archy Moore, she feels that her lighter skin
color places her on a higher social level. Mary has a false sense of
superiority based on skin color.

Mr. Morgan brings Mary a white dress that he says Zeke, an old
African-American man, gave him for her to use for her wedding to Jim.
She refuses, insisting that Hugh Morgan sent her the dress. Mary's
insistence causes Mr. Morgan to become very angry, and he orders Mary

and her Grandmother to leave immediately. Mary finally decides, although reluctantly and hysterically, to marry Jim. Her grandmother then reveals to her that a similar situation had occurred with Henry Morgan and Mary's mother. The grandmother suggests that Mary and Hugh Morgan have the same father.

Mary McLean's plans to marry the son of the owner of the farm are thwarted by her grandmother and Mr. Morgan. Paul Greene, a traditionalist, reverts to the stereotypical situation in which Euro-American men are seduced by young African-American females eager to elevate their standard of living and also their social standing within the African-American community. For Mary, in 1900 rural North Carolina, marriage to Hugh Morgan is a way out of her world and into the white world. Mary's naiveté in wishing to move from the quasi-slave class to the slave-owning class has a hollow ring to it. It is implausible that an African-American woman, no matter how white, would expect the Southern, Euro-American scion of a wealthy family to marry her. However, Mary finally does come to the realization that because she is Black and female, she has few options in life and thus is powerless. If marriage will elevate her status, then it must be marriage to an African-American male.

Wishing to advance her standard of living not through a Euro-American male but through a man nonetheless is Cissy Dildine in T. S. Stribling's *Birthright* (1922). Stribling, born in Clifton, Tennessee, was a journalist, teacher, and lawyer before winning the Pulitzer Prize in 1933 for *The Store*.

Peter Siner, the African-American protagonist of *Birthright*, has returned to Hooker's Bend, Tennessee, after graduating from Harvard. He intends to start a small school, which he hopes will later become a college. However, everything that he attempts goes wrong, so much so that he becomes the village joke. The only people who sympathize with him are Captain Renfrow, also a Harvard graduate (and probably Peter's father), and Cissie Dildine.

Cissie, who is usually identified in the novel as "the octoroon," is immediately attracted to Peter, a mulatto, because they are both educated, she in Nashville, Tennessee, and he at Harvard. Cissie hopes that Peter will take her away to the North because she finds life in the small, Southern village stifling for several reasons. "Peter, it's hard to be nice in Niggertown."[41] "Nice" in this context means if not celibate, at least sexually discriminate. The difficulty in being "nice" exists in the attitudes of the other villagers toward the African-American women. The racist Euro-Americans had attached certain behaviors, immorality, and subhumanity to the African-Americans. The African-Americans of the village had internalized the qualities assigned to them.

Cissie herself had assimilated some of these beliefs; she was "light-fingered," and she eventually became pregnant by her employer's son. Peter has asked her to marry him, but she refuses because she is pregnant by another man, explaining that if he were anyone else, she would accept his proposal. But now he is more like a Euro-American man, and as an African-American woman she does not meet the requisite moral standards.

Not only had his deceased mother been opposed to Peter's marriage to Cissie, but so had been Captain Renfrow. Captain Renfrow objects because Cissie is "a negress!" To Captain Renfrow, negress carries the implication of immorality. Cissy is not only a negress and a thief but "an animal, a female centaur, a wanton and a strumpet, as all negresses are wantons and strumpets."[42] Cissie understood and accepted the attitudes about her gender and ethnicity. Peter, also, is aware of the disrespect shown to African-American women in his community, but he seems to concur if the woman is not of a particular type.

When Cissie is framed for stealing a brooch from the home of her former lover and arrested, Tump (one of her former suitors) and Peter go to her rescue. When she is released from jail, practicality overcomes idealism. She and Peter marry and leave Hooker's Bend, Tennessee, for Chicago.

Cissie is redeemed by the love of a "good" man and hopes that marriage and the move to the North, where all things seem possible, will allow her to cast aside the image of the slut. But Cissie carries with her all of the Euro-American definitions of African-American women. Implicit in the ending is that in the North, all things are possible. But escape from heritage is impossible; North or South, Cissie will be the African-American slut.

The image of the African-American woman as a slut is usually counterbalanced by the image of the mammy, or the "Aunt Jemima." The stereotypical image of the Aunt Jemima depicted the African-American woman as older, fat, servile, long-suffering, and passive. Historian Herbert Gutman argues in *The Black Family in Slavery and Freedom, 1750–1925* that there is little historical evidence to support that notion.

The typical . . . house servant was a young unmarried black woman. . . . Little evidence indicates the presence of the loyal "mammy" laboring as a servant for white families. Very few elderly black women had such jobs.[43]

Gutman notwithstanding, the image of the Aunt Jemima persisted from pre–Civil War to the 1960s. Aunt Jemima was the prototype of the contented slave:[44] the earth mother, physically strong, dependable and happy, always laughing. She was similar to the fallen woman in that there were always many children around her but never a husband. The fallen woman may have been attractive in her brightly colored clothing, but the mammy was careless with her appearance and personal hygiene; she wore a greasy head rag and too-tight shoes on her huge feet. "Her greatest virtue was of course her love for white folk whom she willingly and passively served."[45] The passive, long-suffering, submissive mammy image was created by Euro-American propagandists to justify that, after all, slavery was not evil. The image seemed to prove that there was a place in the social institution for those who did not resist the system. For whatever reason, the myth has continued and been constantly reinforced in film and literature.

Two particular events crystallized the image in the minds of the American public. First was the publication of Margaret Mitchell's novel, *Gone with the Wind*, and the subsequent movie of the same name in which Hattie McDaniel—by playing a mammy—became the first African-American woman to win an Academy Award. Second was the pancake mix box cover that used the likeness of a mammy-like character known as Aunt Jemima. "She was a broad-bosomed, fat, handkerchief head, gingham-dressed, black mammy who told worried housewives, 'Don' yo' fret none, honey. . . . Jus' follow dese directions for de world's most delicious pancakes.' "[46] She made no selling arguments; her comfortable familiarity simply reminded the public of the product.

The Aunt Jemima or mammy as a literary character is motherly, lovable, and non-threatening. The earliest literary representation of the mammy image is found in Mary Eastman's *Aunt Phillis's Cabin* (1852). This very popular novel, which was written to dilute the influence of Harriet Beecher Stowe's *Uncle Tom's Cabin*, glorified slavery and denounced the abolitionists, although it did attempt to describe slave life. Aunt Phillis is a paragon of virtue: "A tall, dignified bright mulatto, Aunt Phillis ironically stints her own child at her breast and gives preference to the white one."[47]

The apparent preference for the Euro-American child is one of the hallmarks of the mammy, and this preference illustrates another of her characteristics: self-sacrifice. The mammy is the person to whom Euro-American mothers relinquished their children for nursing and care. Because of her position, the mammy frequently had to nurse or show a preference for these children. It is ironic that the very women who have been characterized as loose and immoral are the women to whom Euro-Americans have entrusted their children. However, the symbol is so prevalent in American fiction that William Faulkner dedicated *Go Down Moses* (1940) to his mammy.

To Mammy
CAROLINE BARR
Mississippi
[1840–1940]

Who was born in slavery and who gave to my family a fidelity without stint or calculation of recompense and to my childhood an immeasurable devotion and love.

The remembered love and devotion of the mammy is prominently featured in the writings of many American authors. Joel Chandler Harris created his "Mom Bi: Her Friends and Her Enemies" (1884) and Thomas Nelson Page his Mammy Krenda in *Red Rock* (1898). Kate Chopin's *Bayou Folk* (1894), a collection of short stories set in Louisiana, created La Chatte who, like Mark Twain's Roxy in *Pudd' nhead Wilson* (1896), happily interferes in the affairs of others, although without Roxy's tragic results.

After Emancipation, the love and devotion of the mammy did not change, only the status of the woman who gave the care. During Reconstruction and after, virtually the only employment available to the newly freed former slave women was as domestics. These women had to return to the only skill they had: working in the kitchens and homes of Euro-Americans. W. E. B. Du Bois exposes the situation as demeaning: "The personal degradation of their work is so great that any white man of decency would rather cut his daughter's throat than let her grow up to such a destiny."[48]

The stereotypical characterization of the mammy, then, is as nursemaid to the Euro-American children, whom she loved more than her own; she is unclean, happy, hard-working, submissive. Her name was always prefaced with "Auntie" or "Mammy," yet she referred to her young charges as "Mr." or "Miss."

The mammy character who ostensibly deviated from this pattern is William Faulkner's Dilsey in *The Sound and The Fury* (1929). Apparently drawing on memories of Caroline Barr, Faulkner created in Dilsey a "mammy" figure somewhat unlike her predecessors but nevertheless still a mammy.

Dilsey is the loyal servant-matriarch of the Compsons, and her devotion and care of the Compson children and the Compson family place her squarely in the mammy mold. Her comic style of dress also reinforces the image: "She wore a stiff black straw hat perched upon her turban, and a maroon velvet cape with a border of mangy and anonymous fur above a dress of purple silk."[49] However, there are some differences. As the

Compson children call her by her first name (without a title such as "auntie" or "mammy"), she also calls them by their first names, even after they become adults. She also loves and cares for her own children. She has a husband, Roskus. She is not fat, although she "had been a big woman once but now her skeleton rose, draped loosely in unpadded skin that tightened again upon a paunch almost dropsical."[50]

Like the stereotypical mammy, Dilsey heroically attempts to hold the degenerate, disintegrating Compson family together, but her efforts are ignored by Caroline Compson, to whom she remains the invisible domestic, "a blobby shape without depth."[51] Caroline Compson has failed in her responsibilities as a mother, and Dilsey has made the decision to take over the role of surrogate mother—not cheerfully but through a sense of duty. It is this sense of duty that permeates the character of Dilsey—a responsibility not to her Euro-American employers but a responsibility to her God to comfort those in need.

Comforting is a major function of the mammy, and so is friendship. Katherine Anne Porter's mammy, Nannie, in "The Old Order" and "The Last Leaf" (1934) is the central character in a "powerful if brief study of strong positive cross-racial bonds between two women of the Old South,"[52] as well as a continuation of the mammy image.

Nannie had been bought for twenty dollars at a slave auction as a companion and pet for the "prissy, spoiled, five year old" Miss Sophia Jane. Sophia Jane and Nannie grew up together, and when Sophia Jane was married, Nannie was married, too; Nannie and her new "husband" were given to Sophia Jane as wedding presents. Sophia Jane and Nannie gave birth together, and it became Nannie's task to nurse both babies. But at the birth of Nannie's fourth child, she became ill and Sophia nursed Nannie's baby. Sophia Jane developed an attachment to the child and soon understood that she had cheated herself as a mother by giving her children to another woman to nurse; she resolved never to be cheated again.

Nannie, however, was the one who was cheated. Although her relationship with Sophia Jane seemed reciprocal, Nannie was still a slave. Her skin color had determined her place within a system that dictated immediate obedience to any Euro-American authority. Nannie was not unaware of her station in life—enslaved, poor, uneducated— although she had been a faithful and loyal companion to Sophia Jane. With Emancipation she was finally able, much like Faulkner's Dilsey, to make decisions concerning her personal fate and future.

It pleased Nannie to know that although she was born in slavery, she would not die in it. She was hurt not so much by her condition as by the word *slave*, describing it. *Emancipation* resonated sweetly in her ear.

Freedom had not changed her way of living in any particular manner, but she was proud of having been able to say to Sophia Jane, her owner, "I aim to stay wid you as long as you'll have me."[53]

Eventually, the day of retirement came for Nannie when she could sit in idleness and not answer to anyone. She moved into an abandoned cabin on the property to which her "ex-husband" was not allowed entry. No longer a mammy or a freed slave, she considered herself an independent woman. However, she was not as independent as she assumed. Periodically she would visit the "big house" to restock her cabin and to get some attention. Rather than cross-racial bonding, as has been suggested by Minrose C. Gwin, the stories continue the depiction of the African-American woman as passively accepting her status with little to call her own except the friendship and charity of her Euro-American mistress. Friendship usually occurs between equals, but their relationship is not equal. Sophia Jane *owns* Nannie. Therefore, the relationship of mistress to slave continues even after Emancipation and is intensified with some variations on the theme; however, Nannie is still a slave and must function within that role. She has no control over her choice of husband, her body, her place in society, or her life.

A mammy-like character who seemingly has this type of control is Berenice Sadie Brown in Carson McCullers' *The Member of the Wedding* (1946). Berenice is cook and substitute mother to Frankie Adams, the adolescent heroine of the novel; however, Berenice is not an Aunt Jemima. She is an individual who does not have the lowered self-esteem of previous Aunt Jemima characters. Physically, she fits the mammy image with one exception: "her left eye was bright blue glass."[54]

Berenice's blue eye helps her to define her world. Of African ancestry, living in a small, segregated Southern town, working as a domestic, constantly reminded of "her place," she has to make sense of her life and restructure her situation to suit herself. Berenice's life has been circumscribed by the racist-sexist attitudes of the time, but she has never been defeated. She still dreams of a different and better life, but she is pragmatic, and her willingness to see life and her environment as it is makes her self-assured.

Berenice is not a true mammy; she is the mammy transformed and elevated as a working woman. She loves the Adams family, but she never confuses them with her own family. Berenice is independent, self-sufficient, and self-supporting. She is included here because she performs the domestic chores for the Adams family and cares for Frankie, but Berenice Sadie Brown knows the difference between servant and servitude.

If the servant mammy or Aunt Jemima is the counterpart of the "fallen" African-American woman, then the more recent twin of the "fallen" woman is "Sapphire." Sapphire is malicious, vicious, bitchy, loud, bawdy, domineering, and emasculating.

The emasculating African-American woman and the companion myth of the African-American matriarchy were popularized by Daniel P. Moynihan in his sociopolitical study *The Negro Family: The Case for National Action*. In an essay in *The Black Woman*, Jean Carey Bond and Patricia Peery argue that there are two versions of the matriarchy myth.[55] One is that African-American men historically have failed to protect their families from the affliction of American racism. Even more appalling, African-American men have fallen short in developing strategies for liberation of the African-American people. The conclusion is that African-American men are effeminate and contemptible. Because of their weaknesses, that is, their presumed inability to function as Euro-American men, African-American women must take the masculine role. The other version postulates that African-American men are weak because they have been castrated by African-American women. In this version, African-American women have been employed when African-American men have not. This account overlooks the role that racism has played in the employment of African-Americans. African-American women as employed heads of households are viewed as emasculating. More than just being emasculating, the Sapphire image is based on one of the oldest negative stereotypes of woman: inherently and inescapably evil.

The Sapphire image has been more prevalent in the electronic media than in literature; it probably had its genesis in the character Sapphire on the radio and television program "Amos and Andy." Melvin Patrick Ely observes that

Sapphire was strong-willed and decisive . . . much of whose scolding of her husband was understandable in view of his laziness and dishonesty. Yet her assertiveness often took on the shrill tone of the shrew, and the couple's relationship conformed closely to the stereotype of the female-dominated black family— *sans* children. . . . "Sapphire," in fact, had already become a generic folk term among Afro-Americans for a domineering wife.[56]

This media-generated image of the African-American woman that emerged in the 1930s and 1940s invariably portrayed the Sapphire as obstinate, domineering, and contemptuous of African-American men, who were depicted as oppressed.

Although it had been difficult for African-American men to obtain gainful employment in the post–Civil War era, the most menial labor was not available during and after the Great Depression. African-American women, on the other hand, in both periods were able to work as domestics, cooks, laundresses, and maids. On their meager salaries they were at least capable of providing food, clothing, and shelter for their families. But according to the Euro-American value system, this was the man's job. African-American women were thrust into a pseudo-masculine role by the discriminatory practices of the dominant society. The assumption was that the person who earned and controlled the money also was the person with power within the relationship. If women earned, and presumably controlled, the money, then men were in a subordinate position and thus emasculated. The image of the Sapphire is deeply rooted in anti-female mythology; and as the word *black* has numerous negative connotations, the word *woman* in conjunction with *black* evokes the most pernicious and demonic images. But more than just denigration of the African-American woman, other groups of women have used these characteristics ascribed to her to enhance their own image. The Euro-American woman, for instance, can claim even greater purity and innocence when compared with the African-American woman. Even African-American men are able to justify their abuse of African-American women because of their wickedness.

Barbara Smith suggests in "Doing Research on Black Women" that Sapphire appears quasi-masculine when compared to the ultra-feminine Euro-American woman because Sapphire is strong and independent. This is the source of her emasculating ability, although Sapphire is much the same as the mammy. They both share similar types of employment, domestic work; however, Sapphire is not so much devoted to Euro-Americans as she is unfeminine in her relationships with African-American men. To African-American men, she is cold, hard, and evil.[57] Some male writers readily accepted this Euro-American-created myth with their own embellishments. Eldridge Cleaver, for example, describes the African-American woman as "full of steel, granite-hard and resisting, not soft and submissive like a white woman."[58]

This intractability in the Sapphire stereotype can be seen regularly on television. Marla Gibbs' portrayal of the maid, Florence, on "The Jeffersons" is a good example of the strong-willed, flippant, irreverent, urban African-American woman who has no respect for her male employer. Florence's *raison d'être* is a continual demonstration of her contempt for the weak African-American male. She amply authenticates Edward Mapp's comment that "the thin line between the black mammy and

[Sapphire] may be distinguished largely by whether the old girl is presiding over a white or black household."[59]

Tragic mulatta, Aunt Jemima, loose woman, Sapphire: these are the images of the African-American woman in United States culture. In various forms these images entered literature and became ingrained in the American psyche. These images were begun and maintained for specific reasons, mainly the continued oppression and exploitation of the only group in the United States, with the exception of Native Americans, who cannot be classified as immigrants.

African-Americans were originally brought to the United States as a source of unpaid labor. Once here, different theories about their alleged inferiority, from biblical to biological, evolved, all designed to justify and perpetuate their oppression. The theories were transitory, but the literary images were more permanent.

These literary images were included in the works of leading authors as well as the merely mediocre. These representations seemed to fall into one of several carefully designed categories, but for African-American women, the images were particularly detrimental. History and literature seemed to collude in saying that if women, nature's most beautiful, cultured creatures, behave in this manner (the loose woman, the Sapphire), then civilized society must be protected from these "subhuman" creatures.

With the coming of the Civil Rights Movement of the 1960s, it would seem that some of these images should have disappeared. They did not; they were merely revamped. A change in the existing social structure was only cosmetic, not revolutionary. The African-American community was still attacked through its women, particularly in the media. The loose woman has now become the "welfare queen" and the producer of crack babies. The Sapphire is the poverty-stricken female head of household. Only the lovable, nurturing mammy seems to have disappeared.

NOTES

1. bell hooks, *Ain't I a Woman. Black Women and Feminism* (Boston: South End Press, 1981), 16.

2. Dorothy Sterling, ed., *We Are Your Sisters. Black Women in the Nineteenth Century* (New York: W. W. Norton and Company, 1984), 19.

3. hooks, 16–17.

4. Louis Ruchames, *Racial Thought in America, from the Puritans to Abraham Lincoln* (New York: Grosset and Dunlap, 1969), 439.

5. Nancy M. Tischler, *Black Masks. Negro Characters in Modern Southern Fiction* (University Park, PA: The Pennsylvania State University Press, 1969), 64.

6. Robert Staples, *The Black Woman in America. Sex, Marriage and the Family* (Chicago: Nelson-Hall Publishers, 1973), 10.

7. Thomas Gosset, *Race. The History of an Idea in America* (Dallas: Southern Methodist University Press, 1963).

8. Judith R. Berzon, *The Mulatto Character in American Fiction* (New York: New York University Press, 1978), 13.

9. An archetype is the dominant embodiment of an idea or kind of person that rises in literature, attracts conscientious responses, recurs as thematic motif in subsequent manifestations, and acquires mythic dimensions as demanded by cultural needs. Catherine J. Starke, *Black Portraiture in American Fiction. Stock Characters, Archetypes, and Individuals* (New York: Basic Books, Inc., 1971), 88. An archetype is the original; the stereotype is a repeated copy of the archetype with modifications.

10. James F. Cooper, *The Last of the Mohicans* (Twickenham, England: The Felix Gluck Press, 1856), 55.

11. Sterling Brown, *The Negro in American Fiction* (New York: Arno Press and the New York Times, 1969), 32.

12. Miscegenation and *partus sequitur ventrem*, that is, the child inherits the condition of the mother, "whitened" the slave population. Joel Williamson, in *New People. Miscegenation and Mulattoes in the United States* (New York: The Free Press, 1980, 62), writes: "The great fact about mulattoes that emerges from a comparison of the census of 1860 with that of 1850 is a massive increase in the number of mulattoes who were slaves. During the decade of the 1850s slavery was becoming whiter, visibly so and with amazing rapidity. White people were enslaving themselves, as it were, in the form of their children and their children's children. While black slavery increased in numbers only 19.8 percent in the decade, mulatto slavery rose by an astonishing 66.9 percent."

13. In some states, there were attempts to establish the mulatto as a third caste. However, the idea never became widespread.

Winthrop Jordan, *White over Black. American Attitudes Toward the Negro, 1550–1812* (Chapel Hill: The University of North Carolina Press, 1968, 169):

In 1765 the colony of Georgia . . . actually provided that free mulatto and mustee [the offspring of a Native American and an African] might be naturalized as white men, by the legislature and be endowed with "all Rights, Privileges, Powers and Immunities whatsoever which any person born of British parents" could have, except the right to vote and sit in the Commons House of Assembly. Thus a degree of citizenship was begrudgingly extended to free mulattoes.

C. Vann Woodward, *The Strange Career of Jim Crow* (New York: Oxford University Press, 1966), 102: "South Carolina for a time segregated a third caste by establishing separate schools for mulatto as well as for white and Negro children."

Paul R. Spickard, *Mixed Blood. Intermarriage and Ethnic Identity in Twenti-eth-Century America* (Madison: The University of Wisconsin Press, 1989, 316):

A third separate group consists of communities of people of mixed Black, White, and Native American ancestry, located mainly in isolated parts of the rural South. Groups such as the Melungeons and Lumbee constituted something of a curiosity in the two-cat-egory American racial system. Most existed as separate communities for many genera-tions. Nearly all called themselves Indians and claimed only Native American and White ancestry, yet neighbors and social scientists insisted they had significant Black parentage as well. They were an anomaly, for there was no place for them in the two-caste system. For purposes of segregation, they tended to be regarded as honorary Whites, although sometimes they were segregated with Blacks or kept to themselves.

14. Colonel Moore's pursuit of Cassie may seem unusual since she is his daughter, but its counterpart exists in reality. Joel Williamson (p. 55) writes of the case of Patrick and Peggy, lovers who murdered their master. One witness said that the deceased, to whom Peggy belonged, had had a disagreement with Peggy and generally kept her confined, chained to a block and locked up in his meat house; that he believed the reason why the deceased had treated Peggy in this way was that Peggy would not consent to intercourse with him; and that he had heard the deceased say that if Peggy did not agree to his request in that way, he would beat her almost to death, that he would barely leave the life in her, and would send her to New Orleans. According to the witness, Peggy said she would not yield to his request because the deceased was her father, and she could not do a thing of that sort with her father. the witness heard the deceased say to Peggy that if she did not consent, he would make the witness and Patrick hold her, to enable him to effect his object.

15. J. Noel Heermance, *William Wells Brown and Clotelle. A Portrait of the Artist in the First Negro Novel* (np: Archon Books, 1969), 74.

16. Brown, 49.

17. Starke, 65.

18. William S. Braithwaite, "The Negro in American Fiction," in *Black Expression*, Addison Gayle, Jr., ed. (New York: Weybright and Talley, 1969), 171.

19. *Creole* can be defined as a person of mixed Spanish and African ancestry or French and African ancestry, but this definition does not contain all the ramifications of the word. See Virginia R. Dominguez, *White by Definition. Social Classification in Creole Louisiana* (New Brunswick, NJ: Rutgers Univer-sity Press, 1986).

20. The reappearance of characteristics of some remote ancestor that have been absent in intervening generations. For an interesting short story on atavism, see "Désirée's Baby," in Kate Chopin's *Bayou Folk*.

21. William Dean Howells, *An Imperative Duty* (New York: Harper and Brothers, 1892), 16–17.

22. Ibid., 145.

23. Ibid., 149.

24. J. C. Furnas, *Goodbye to Uncle Tom* (New York: William Sloan Associates, 1956), 140.

25. Gerda Lerner, ed., *Black Women in White America. A Documentary History* (New York: Pantheon Books, 1972), 163.

26. Ibid., 193.

27. hooks, 52.

28. Walter White, *The Rope and the Faggot. A Biography of Judge Lynch* (New York: Arno Press and The New York Times, 1969, 1929), 66.

29. Calvin Hernton, *Sex and Racism in America* (New York: Grove Press, 1965), 125.

30. Mel Watkins and Jay David, *To Be a Black Woman. Portraits in Fact and Fiction* (New York: William Morrow and Company, Inc., 1970), dust jacket.

31. Paula Giddings, *When and Where I Enter. The Impact of Black Women on Race and Sex in America* (New York: Bantam Books, 1984), 46.

32. William Goodell, *The American Slave Code* (New York: Arno Press and The New York Times, 1969), 86.

33. Starke, 146.

34. DuBose Heywood, *Porgy* (Dunwoody, GA: Norman S. Berg Publisher, 1925), 41.

35. Ibid., 77.

36. Dorothy and DuBose Heywood, *Mamba's Daughters* (New York: Farrar and Rinehart, 1939), 63.

37. Tischler, 65.

38. Heywood and Heywood, 140.

39. Ibid., 102.

40. Robert Hill, *The Strength of Black Families* (New York: Emerson Hall Publishers, Inc., 1976), 5–6.

41. T. S. Stribling, *Birthright* (Delmar, NY: Scholars' Facsimiles and Reprints, 1987, 1922), 94.

42. Ibid., 229.

43. Herbert G. Gutman, *The Black Family in Slavery and Freedom, 1750–1925* (New York: Pantheon Books, 1976), 443.

44. Sterling Brown characterized the stereotypes of African-Americans appearing in Euro-American fiction as the contented slave, the wretched freedman, the comic Negro, the brute Negro, the local color Negro, the tragic mulatto, and the exotic primitive.

45. hooks, 84.

46. Daniel J. Leab, *From Sambo to Superspade. The Black Experience in Motion Pictures* (Boston: Houghton Mifflin Co., 1975), 98.

47. Starke, 126.

48. W. E. B. Du Bois, "The Servant in the House," in *Darkwater. Voices from within the Veil* (New York: Harcourt Brace and Howe, 1920), 116.

49. William Faulkner, *The Sound and the Fury* (New York: Harcourt Brace and Co., 1929), 281.

50. Ibid., 282.

51. Ibid., 288.

52. Minrose C. Gwin, *Black and White Women. The Peculiar Sisterhood in American Literature* (Knoxville, TN: The University of Tennessee Press, 1985), 178.

53. Katherine Anne Porter, *The Collected Stories of Katherine Anne Porter* (New York: Harcourt, Brace and World, 1965), 334.

54. Carson McCullers, *The Member of the Wedding* (New York: Bantam Books, 1946), 3.

55. Jean Carey Bond and Patricia Peery, "Is the Black Male Castrated?" in *The Black Woman. An Anthology*, Toni Cade, ed. (New York: New American Library, 1970), 115.

56. Melvin Patrick Ely, *The Adventures of Amos 'n' Andy. A Social History of an American Phenomenon* (New York: The Free Press, 1991), 208.

57. Barbara Smith, "Doing Research on Black American Women," *Women's Studies Newsletter* 4 (Spring 1976): 4.

58. Eldridge Cleaver, *Soul on Ice* (New York: Dell Publishing Co., 1968), 159.

59. Edward Mapp, "Black Women in Films," *Black Scholar* 4 (March/April 1973): 43.

Chapter Three

The Female Response: Harriet E. Wilson to Alice Walker

As early as 1892 African-American feminist Anna Julia Cooper was urging the study of Black women because Black women's experiences were very different from those of Black men. However, until the 1960s when African-American women began to study themselves, the voice of the African-American male has been thought to be the voice of the African-American woman as well. "Regardless of class, black women are defined in this nation as a group *distinct* from black men and *distinct* from white people *only* because of the double jeopardy of race and sex."[1] Although African-American men and African-American women share a common history, the women have faced and continue to face triple oppression: of race, class, and gender. But although the Abolitionists, Civil Rights leaders, and the giants of African-American literature (until recently) have been men, African-American writing began with a woman.

Lucy Terry Prince (1730–1821) is considered the first African-American poet. She earned this distinction with the publication of her only known poem, "Bars Fight" (1796). Inspired by an ambush of two families in Deerfield, Massachusetts, by sixty Native Americans, the poem did not deal with African-Americans or the slave experience. The early, although limited, literary exploration of the slave experience was left to Phillis Wheatley (1753?–1784), the first African-American and the second woman, following Anne Bradstreet, to publish a volume of poetry. But as Ann Allen Shockley says, "She made no strong protests against slavery and because of this, she has been denigrated by some African-American contemporaries."[2] A careful examination of her poetry reveals, however, that she was aware of her race and circumstances, and that knowledge did not allow her to make strong protests. The conclusion arrived at by Richard Wright, that "she was so fully at one with white colonial culture that she developed innocently, free to give utterance to what she felt without the humiliating pressure of the color line,"[3] may be dismissed considering Wright's alienation from African-American culture.

Although Wheatley may not have emphasized her slave condition in her writing, her insight into her ethnicity, gender, and condition can be seen in poems such as "Brought from Africa to America," "To the University of Cambridge...," and "An Hymn to Humanity."[4] Early critics have referred to her poetry as "smoothly crafted, but artificial and imitative of Pope and the neoclassicists"[5] and have said that she "must be considered a minor English poet . . . whose interest for Afro-American literature is minimal."[6] In spite of such criticism, Alice Walker maintains that within a repressive, racist colonial society, she preserved for her descendants "the notion of song" in the only manner she could.[7]

Many African-American women began to preserve their histories and identities through writing in the late eighteenth and early nineteenth centuries. Some of these early writers were Ann Plato (1820–?), Zilpha Elaw (?–?), Jarena Lee (1783–?) and Nancy Gardener Prince (1799–?).[8] This group, including Lucy Terry and Phillis Wheatley, may have ignored slavery or glossed over it lightly in their writings, perhaps in fear of alienating their Euro-American audiences or publishers. Despite their curious omissions, later women writers would confront the issue of slavery, the status of African-Americans in United States society, and specifically their images as women. The most significant of those images, as noted in the previous chapter, are the tragic mulatto, the Aunt Jemima, the "loose woman," and the Sapphire. African-American women refuted these images, confronted their history, and recreated their "selves" in their writings.

Many of the early writers who explored the issues of their status and images as African-American women did so in the form of slave narratives. An exception to the Southern slave narrative was Harriet E. Wilson's *Our Nig; or, Sketches from the Life of a Free Black, in a Two-Story White House, North. Showing That Slavery's Shadows Fall Even There* (1859). This was the semi-fictionalized autobiographical account of the life of a free African-American woman in the North. The work predates William Wells Brown's *Clotelle: A Tale of the Southern States* (1867), which was once regarded as the first published long work by an African-American. That honor now belongs to Harriet E. Wilson. Moreover, Wilson holds the distinction of being "one of the first two black women writers to publish a novel in any language."9

Our Nig is the story of Frado (Alfrado), the daughter of a free African-American male, Jim, and a Euro-American woman, Mag Smith. Mag has been abandoned by the community because, prior to her marriage to Jim, she had given birth to an illegitimate child. After the death of her husband, Mag, unable to support her children, deserts them. At the age of six, Frado is indentured to the Bellmont family. Here, she is ruled over by the "she-devil" Mrs. Bellmont and her equally vicious daughter, Mary. The brutal, racist relationship between Frado and Mrs. Bellmont becomes the central theme of the novel. Finally, at the age of eighteen, Frado is released from indenture, but because of overwork and physical abuse, her health is broken.

Frado leaves the Bellmonts, learns a trade, and falls in love with and marries Samuel, who postures as an escaped slave. Samuel deserts Frado and their child and eventually dies of yellow fever in New Orleans. In an effort to support the child, Frado, like Wilson, writes her fictionalized autobiography. But it is published too late; the child dies. Published one month before John Brown's raid on Harper's Ferry and at a time when the two most urgent social issues were the rights of African-Americans and the rights of women, Wilson's book should have been a success. But it was not because anti-Black sentiment was not geographically systematized, an actuality that the Abolitionists did not want generally known. Although Mrs. Bellmont was Northern, she was "wholly imbued with *southern* principles."10 But the Southern principles that had so influenced Wilson's mistress had also affected the entire country.

Thus *Our Nig*, published in 1859, was not reprinted until 1983. Henry Louis Gates in his introduction speculates that the "boldness of her [Wilson's] themes" caused its obscurity. In addition to a racial indictment of the North, there were the portrayal of an interracial marriage and the use of the pejorative *nigger*, for the title and the author.11 There is another reason why the book may have been ignored. Ann Allen Shockley speculates that it may have been overlooked because of the misidentification of its writer. She points out that "Monroe N. Work, in his mammoth *A Bibliography of the Negro in Africa and America* (1928) . . . lists Mrs. H. E. Wilson under the heading of 'Novels by White Authors Relating to the Negro.' "12

Whatever the rationale for its obscurity, *Our Nig* is important for reasons other than its being the first long work written by an African-American woman. The work explicitly demonstrates that racial prejudice existed both North and South—that Northern Euro-American women as well as those in the South enforced the rules of the patriarchy and that Euro-American women did form sexual liaisons with African-American men. In addition, *Our Nig* is an early example of the African-American working mother and wife, a single parent, and the first in a long line of African-American women who have been abandoned by their men.

The more typical slave narrative, which sometimes involves liaisons between a Euro-American male and his African-American female slave, is found in Harriet Ann Jacobs' (pseud. Linda Brent, 1813–1897) *Incidents in the Life of a Slave Girl, Written by Herself* (1861). Although "12 percent of these antebellum publications [slave narratives] were by women who escaped to the North and had their life stories published . . . and a good number of these were written by others,"[13] Jacobs wrote her own narrative, as authenticated by her biographer, Jean Fagin Yellin.

Approximately eighty years before Anne Frank hid from her Nazi oppressors in a Dutch attic, Linda Brent fled to her grandmother's attic to escape the unreasonable jealousy of Mrs. Flint and the unwanted sexual attentions of her owner, Dr. Flint. With the assertion, "Slavery is terrible for men; but it is far more terrible for women,"[14] Brent clearly indicates the theme of her narrative: the special horrors of slavery for women.

When Brent was fourteen years old, Dr. Flint had informed her of his intentions of establishing her as his concubine. To elude Dr. Flint's attentions, Brent deliberately chooses one of the Euro-American neighbors, Mr. Sands, as a lover because "it seems less degrading to give one's self than to submit to compulsion."[15] Later, she appealed for a change in the moral standards as applied to slave women. She argued that enslaved women cannot be held accountable to the same arbitrary moral standards as free women.

She bore two children, Benjamin and Ellen, for Mr. Sands. Brent is clearly aware of the choices she has made, but her enslaved condition precludes any other decision. It is only when Dr. Flint decides to sell her children that Brent determines that she must escape. She convinces Mr. Sands to purchase the children. He does so and entrusts Benjamin and Ellen to Brent's grandmother.

After seeing that her children are safe, Brent goes first to a kindly Euro-American woman for shelter and later moves into her grandmother's attic. After seven years in hiding, Brent finally escapes to the North. In the North, Brent is not completely free; the Fugitive Slave Act of 1850 is in effect, a law that gave the federal government almost unlimited power for the apprehension and return of runaway slaves. Dr. Flint makes several trips to New York in an effort to regain his property, but eventually Brent is able to purchase her freedom. With the help of Brent's brother, her children escape via the Underground Railroad and join her in New York. Although Brent follows the patterns that are standard for female slave narratives, she deviates significantly from the depictions in most of the narratives. None of the "curious omissions" of many of the female slave narratives is present. Brent very clearly outlines the sexual exploitation prepared for her by Dr. Flint. Like many of the narrators, Brent experiences matraphobia, that is, she does not want her daughter exposed to the evils of slavery. She is an outraged mother, not a mammy. She uses her nurturing for her own children rather than for the Euro-American family that owns her. Additionally, the grandmother is a free person of color with powerful, influential Euro-American friends who are in a position to help Brent.

Brent, as a mulatta, differs significantly from the tragic mulatta created by Euro-American writers. While she is beautiful, rebellious, ambitious, and independent, she is not a victim struggling to escape the sexual grips of a licentious Euro-American male. Nor does she reject her "African-ness"; instead, she is firm in her commitment to her ethnicity.

With the abolition of slavery and the onset of Reconstruction, African-American women were faced not only with the effect of their images but the survival of African-Americans as a people. Now added to these concerns were the betterment of the race and the improvement of their condition as women. Emancipation was followed by Reconstruction and segregation; thus the 1880s and the 1890s became a difficult time for African-Americans. There was the installation of Jim Crow laws across the South and, in other areas, disfranchisement, peonage, and mob violence in the form of lynching.[16]

From the end of the Civil War in 1865 until the end of the nineteenth century, thousands of African-American men, women, and children were lynched, for a variety of reasons. Most of those lynched were men usually charged with the rape of Euro-American women. This charge slandered not only African-American men but also African-American women. It was believed that the "immoral behavior" of African-American wives, mothers, and daughters was at the root of the so-called lascivious behavior of the race. The "immoral behavior" coincided with one of the prevailing stereotypes of the African-American woman as a slut, a woman readily available to any man. It would seem that this "immoral behavior" would have had the opposite effect on the behavior of African-American men, since many women were already available to them, but racism is seldom logical.

In addition to the rape of Euro-American women, other reasons occasionally given for lynchings were the possibility of African-American riots and fear of domination. However, historians have pointed out that no alleged rapes were reported prior to or during the Civil War when slaves were left in charge of Euro-American families and property. Other historians have suggested that the lynchings occurred because of the resentfulness of new African-American freedoms guaranteed by the Civil Rights Act of 1875. Perhaps the actual reason for the lynchings was to continue the oppression of African-Americans in order to maintain a supply of cheap labor and reinforce a rigid caste system.

These lynchings continued unchallenged until in Memphis on March 9, 1892, three African-American men, Calvin McDowell, Will Stewart, and Thomas Moss, were taken from the county jail and lynched. Moss was a friend of an African-American journalist, Ida B. Wells (pseudonym, Iola). In reality Wells' friend Moss died because his business competed with a nearby Euro-American business. Until the lynchings of Moss and his partners, Wells had apparently believed the reports of rape as one of the reasons for lynchings. However, after the lynching of her friend, Wells wrote an editorial for the *Memphis Free Speech and Headlight,* an African-American newspaper, in which she boldly stated that the connection of African-American men with the rape of Euro-American women was dishonest hyperbole. She ended the editorial with, "If Southern white men are not careful, they will over-reach themselves and . . . a conclusion will then be reached which will be very damaging to the moral reputation of their women."[17] Luckily, Wells was out of the city when local Euro-Americans destroyed her office and temporarily disrupted her livelihood. Nevertheless, Wells continued her newspaper career with anti-lynching as its focus, although away from Memphis.

Wells' aggressive journalistic style stimulated other African-American women to join the anti-lynching crusade. Wells' agitation laid the foundation for the beginning of the African-American women's club movement. Along with W.E.B. Du Bois, she was a founder of the National Association for the Advancement of Colored People. A militant womanist,[18] in Chicago in 1913 she organized the Alpha Suffrage Club, the first suffrage group composed of African-American women.

In addition in racism, African-American women had to confront the issue of sexism. While nineteenth-century middle-class Euro-American women stayed at home in a subservient role, African-American women, perhaps, were more acutely aware of sexist oppression than any other group.

During the late nineteenth century, many African-American women changed the focus of their writing from anti-slavery to sexism and racism. However, in their fiction, the theme of sexism was not prominent. Carole McAlpine Watson writes that the fiction of African-American women during this period was comprised of "romantic tales [which] focused on black heroes and heroines of saintlike virtue."[19] Perhaps the best example of this type of fiction is Frances Ellen Watkins Harper's *Iola Leroy; or Shadows Uplifted* (1892), at one time incorrectly considered the first novel by an African-American woman.[20]

Harper was one of the leading figures of both the Abolitionist and feminist movements, writing[21] and lecturing in defense of her race and gender. In *Iola Leroy*, Harper elaborates on the most pressing needs of the African-American community. *Iola Leroy* is the tale of an octoroon who until the age of eighteen was unaware of her African ancestry.

Iola Leroy's father is a Mississippi planter who manumits his favorite female slave and educates her in the North. After she graduates from college, Mr. Leroy marries her, and they return to Mississippi. Mr. Leroy confides his wife's true racial background to only one person, his cousin Lorraine. When Mr. Leroy dies of yellow fever, Lorraine, in connivance with a local judge, has the marriage contract and the manumission papers rescinded. Iola, her siblings, and her mother are remanded to slavery. Iola is sold many times, always to licentious men who buy her for her beauty. Because of her background—socialization as a Euro-American, rich, educated—she has difficulty adjusting to slavery. Iola's virtue is constantly in jeopardy; she spends much of her short time in slavery successfully fending off lascivious slave owners.

Finally, she is rescued by escaped slaves. After her rescue, she works as a nurse for the Union Army, where a Euro-American, Dr. Gresham, asks her to marry him, even though he is aware of her biraciality. Because of the knowledge of her African ancestry, she refuses. After the war, she goes in search of her family members, finds them, and eventually marries another octoroon, Dr. Frank Latimer.

It is the woman, Iola Leroy, around whom Harper constructed her novel. Harper's image of Iola is a direct refutation of many of the negative images of the African-American woman found in Euro-American fiction. She is not a tragic mulatta. She does not deny her heritage, nor does she prefer death to living as an African-American, as her sister does. She is unlike her brother Harry, who lapses into a long coma upon being informed of his potential slave status. Iola Leroy is not a mammy; she is a slim, beautiful woman who is not presented in a motherly, nurturing role. She is not a "loose" woman, nor is she brazen or bawdy; therefore, as a highly principled Christian woman, Harper emphasizes, she does not deserve the traditional barbaric treatment of an enslaved woman. Iola decides to seek employment, in direct contradiction of the tenets of the cult of true womanhood, and at the same time calls attention to one of the many cultural differences between African-American and Euro-American women:[22] "I think that every woman should have some skill or art which would insure her at least a comfortable support. I believe there would be less unhappy marriages if labor were more honored among women."[23] Harper seems to be echoing one of her contemporaries, Anna Julia Cooper (1859–1964), who wrote that women should be prepared to earn their own living "because it renders women less dependent on the marriage relation for physical support (which, by the way, does not always accompany it)."[24]

Iola Leroy, as Barbara Christian points out, "is an important novel . . . because it so clearly delineates the relationship between the images of black women . . . and the novelist's struggle to refute these images."[25] The struggle to refute the stereotypical images of African-American women was continued by other women writers, most notably Amelia E. Johnson (1858–1922)[26] and Pauline Hopkins (1859–1930). Hopkins, one of the most prolific writers[27] of this period, until recently has been overlooked by scholars and critics. She worked as a stenographer until her recognition as a writer of fiction at age forty. She was also literary editor of the *Colored American*, a popular magazine of the time. She served in this position, supporting the magazine's anti–Booker T. Washington stance from 1903 until 1904 when the publication was purchased by a group of Washington's followers and she was replaced.[28]

Hopkins is being rediscovered through reprints of her major novel, *Contending Forces: A Romance Illustrative of Negro Life North and South* (1900). Hopkins is explicit that the use of fiction "is a record of growth and development from generation to generation. . . . We must ourselves develop the men and women who will faithfully portray the inmost thoughts and feelings of the Negro with all the fire and romance which lie dormant in our history."[29]

Hopkins sought to portray these thoughts and feelings of African-American people in her novel, although her thought on societal codes of feminine morality echoes the earlier position of Harriet Jacobs' Linda Brent. Hopkins, through her characters, insists that African-American women must be judged differently from Euro-American women. Slavery must constantly be understood as a causative factor when determining the standards of female morality.

It is in the characterization of Sappho Clark that Hopkins creates a strong, independent African-American woman. In some ways Sappho Clark, a mulatta, is similar to previous mulatta characters, but one of her distinctions is that she must work for pay as a stenographer. She must bring her work home because the Euro-American employees refuse to share an office with her.

Although Sappho is admired by both the men and the women with whom she comes into contact, she is particularly admired by the boarding house maid, Dora, who proudly announces that she will "generally accept whatever the men tell me as right."[30] Dora's relationship with Sappho causes the maid to reassess her previous negative ideas on the importance of female relationships.

Throughout *Contending Forces*, Hopkins continually suggests that African-American women must be supportive of one another. Thus, there is an emphasis not only on the effects of racism but also on sexism. She also implies that for African-American women to succeed and survive in the United States, it is imperative that they confront their history and not deny it.

From the turn of the century and the publication of Hopkins' major works until World War I, the United States progressed rapidly. The country became an imperialistic and industrial nation competing strongly with European nations. But for African-Americans, these years were some of the most formidable that they had yet faced.

Although the incidents of lynchings had declined, they nonetheless continued. Lynchings, injustice in the Southern courts, disfranchisement, a decline in cotton prices, and natural disasters led to a migration by African-Americans from the rural South to the urban North. Once established in the North, African-Americans were faced with more subtle forms of racism. But because the North was rapidly becoming more industrialized, there was more and better paid employment available. In spite of the northward migration and better employment opportunities, the societal position and stereotypical images of African-American women remained unchanged. African-American women writers, however, began to be recognized in the movement referred to as the Harlem Renaissance, or the New Negro Movement, usually dated circa 1924.[31] This movement began at this particular time because of two factors, according to historian John Hope Franklin: "the keener realization of injustice and the improvement of the capacity for expression."[32] This capacity was apparent in all facets of creativity: music, art, and literature.

It was in literature that African-American women excelled. Novelists Jessie Redmon Fauset,[33] Zora Neale Hurston, and Nella Larsen; poets Georgia Douglas Johnson[34] and Clara Ann Thompson;[35] and playwrights Katherine Davis Tillman[36] and Eulalie Spence[37] contributed greatly to what was essentially a male-dominated movement.

Male privilege contributed as much to the masculine domination of the movement as the fact that many of the women writers thought themselves restricted to writing genteel, straitlaced novels about African-Americans with middle-class backgrounds, manners, and values. During this time there was an intense debate among the intelligentsia concerning how the African-American should be portrayed in fiction. Langston Hughes blasted the "Nordicized Negro intelligentsia" for demanding that African-American artists "be respectable, write about nice people [and] show how good [African-American people] are."[38] Nella Larsen seemingly agreed with Hughes and broke, to some extent, with the tradition of women's novels by creating a heroine who was a sexual being.

Larsen (1893?–1964) was born in Chicago to a West Indian father and a Danish mother. After her father deserted the family, the mother remarried a Euro-American and had other children. After the remarriage, Larsen's childhood became very difficult. She was sent away to study at the high school at Fisk University in Nashville, Tennessee. Later, she audited classes at the University of Copenhagen (Denmark), and in New York she earned a certificate in library science and a nursing degree. Larsen published two novels, *Quicksand* (1928) and *Passing* (1929). *Quicksand* is the story of Helga Crane, a woman whose fictional life closely mirrors the real life of Nella Larsen. The novel opens with Helga, the daughter of a West Indian gambler and a Danish mother, considering resigning her position as a teacher at a small Southern African-American college, Naxos. She was not happy, nor could she conform to Naxos' expectations because she was aware of her sensuality. She knew that if she acknowledged this, it would contradict her image as a lady.

At Naxos, being or becoming a lady is very important; as Miss MacGooden, the dormitory matron, constantly reminds her charges, it is necessary to "act like ladies and not like savages from the backwoods."[39] To many African-Americans, like Miss MacGooden, being a lady meant not only being virtuous but also avoiding bright colors, being quiet and unassuming, and strictly following traditional Euro-American middle-class guidelines. Miss MacGooden has followed the strictures for becoming a lady, but she has never married, nor does she intend to, because "there were . . . things in the matrimonial state that were . . . entirely too repulsive for a lady of delicate and sensitive nature to submit to."[40]

Helga is the antithesis of Miss MacGooden. Although she is constantly reminded that she is a "lady [with] dignity and breeding," she realizes that being a lady conflicts with her knowledge of self, a conflict that Naxos methodically reinforces. Naxos, the college where Helga is so miserable, is attempting to erase all vestiges of African-American life and culture from its students.

Notice that *Naxos* is an anagram of *Saxon*, a further indication of the school's tendencies. It is also Larsen's first indication of the direction the novel will take: a criticism of the hypocrisy of the African-American middle-class with its imitation of Euro-American middle-class values. An example of this hypocrisy is Helga's friend, Anne Grey. Anne Grey hates all Euro-Americans and everything they represent, yet at the same time she loves everything African-American. Yet paradoxically, she despises African-American speech, food, dress, and manners, and she slavishly imitates Euro-American clothes, manners, and ways of living. Like the Euro-Americans that she despises, she prefers Euro-American entertainers and artists to African-American: Pavlova to Florence Mills, John McCormack to Taylor Gordon, and Walter Hampden to Paul Robeson. For the same reasons that Anne Grey rejects all aspects of African-American life, Naxos is suffocating to Helga because it lacks humanity, racial pride, and the will to deviate from the philosophy of its Euro-American benefactors.

Helga leaves Naxos and goes to Chicago where she is offered employment as a domestic, the only work available to an African-American woman. Eventually she is befriended and hired as a speech writer for Mrs. Hayes-Rore, a "race" woman, whose livelihood is gained by traveling the country lecturing about African-Americans. Helga accompanies Mrs. Hayes-Rore to New York where she observes and participates in the upper-middle-class social life of Harlem, but she is as unhappy in New York as she was at Naxos.

Upon receiving a check for five thousand dollars from her Danish uncle who had earlier denied her as a family member because of her biraciality, Helga takes the uncle's advice and travels to Copenhagen, where she has wealthy relatives. Their social position allows her to move easily within Danish upper-class society, where she is courted by a well-known artist, Axel Olsen. Helga ultimately rejects his proposal of marriage because she cannot marry a European. As Deborah McDowell indicates, Helga "implies . . . an awareness of her legacy of rape and concubinage at the hands of white men, a legacy which compels her to decline Olsen's . . . marriage proposal."[41]

There is more in question than this rape and concubinage. There is also the question of Helga's portrait by Olsen, which exposes an aspect of Helga that she has been struggling to suppress, her sexuality. The painting pictures her apparently as Olsen saw her—a carnal, exotic primitive. Now her sensuality becomes her primary focus, and after she hears African-American spirituals at a concert, that focus is joined to her race. Helga realizes that she is lonely not for the United States but rather for African-Americans. She returns to New York to the African-American people about whom she has had such ambivalent attitudes. After two years in Denmark, she understands that she is inextricably tied to African-Americans.

Helga now accepts her race[42] and her sexuality. She makes a sexual advance at the husband of her friend, Anne Grey, but is rebuffed. In her anger at his rejection, she runs off and wanders into a fundamentalist church, where she meets the Reverend Mr. Pleasant Green. She is seduced by Reverend Green, marries him, and returns with him to rural Alabama.

It is in Alabama that her sexual nature contributes to her desolation. Although she comes to despise her husband, she looks forward to the nights she spends with him. She has three children in quick succession, and with the birth of the fourth, she nearly dies. During her period of recuperation, Helga has her nurse read Anatole France's "The Procurator of Judea." As McDowell notes, "This popular short story is regarded as anti-Christian and blasphemous. . . . Larsen uses the short story to blast the role of Christianity in the oppression of women."[43] As the novel ends, Helga is pregnant with her fifth child, whose birth will probably lead to her death.

Helga is not the tragic mulatta of Euro-American fiction. There was never a question of her identity, and the African-American community was always the locus of her search for individuality. She discovers that a European community is an alien environment for her.

Critics often have cited the tragic mulatta and racism as the dominant themes in *Quicksand*. But with the development of a feminist consciousness on the part of many critics, other dimensions must be considered. Helga's difficulties are more the consequence of sexism than of racism. According to Hortense Thornton, "Helga Crane was a woman living in a male chauvinistic society wherein social roles, including sexual behavior, were, and still are to a great extent defined by men and by women who accept male dominance."[44]

Thus, Helga Crane is defined, accepted, or rejected by men. Larsen understands the prevailing image of African-American women as sexually indiscriminate and their position and role as women within their community. As a member of the African-American middle class, it became Larsen's obligation to fight against the negative stereotypes by having Helga repress her sexual feelings. But in trying to produce an accurate picture of one African-American woman, it became essential for Larsen to clarify Helga's struggle to cling to outmoded, spurious traditions.

While Helga might seem to be neurotic with her restless wanderings and mood swings, in the end she is trapped by her womb and the same feelings she sought to deny. Larsen implies that female sexuality must be controlled lest the preconceived idea of the loose African-American woman, which began in slavery, be accepted as representative of all. Female sexuality is somewhat more acceptable within the boundaries of marriage. Still, Larsen is in accordance with other women writers who seem to argue that marriage represents a type of death for women. Hence, the suffocation implied in the title.

Nella Larsen was not the only woman writer of the Harlem Renaissance who attempted to present insight into different types of African-American women. During the Harlem Renaissance, African-American writers tended to concentrate on the developing Northern, urban middle class in an effort to explain to their Euro-American readers that there were few differences between the two groups. In the meantime, the "folk," the common or working-class African-American, was all but forgotten. Writing somewhat after the Harlem Renaissance, Zora Neale Hurston in her novel *Their Eyes Were Watching God* (1937) changed the focus from African-Americans in the urban North to the "folk" in the rural South.

Zora Neale Hurston (1903?–1960) was born in the African-American community of Eatonville, Florida. Her mother died when Hurston was nine years old, leaving her to spend her formative years with various relatives. As a teenager, she left her family and took a variety of jobs. Eventually she arrived in Baltimore, where she completed her secondary education. She attended Howard University in Washington, D.C., and subsequently graduated from Barnard College. After graduation from Barnard, she studied anthropology at Columbia University under Franz Boas. Hurston was one of the most prolific writers of the Harlem Renaissance. She collected and compiled African-American folklore, wrote short stories, essays, plays, and novels.[45] Her most popular work is a novel, *Their Eyes Were Watching God.*

Their Eyes Were Watching God is the story of Janie Mae Crawford who in flashback narrates her experiences to her friend, Phoeby. Classism, sexism, and personal evolution are areas that Hurston explores in the novel. Jay Walker explains that "Janie seems to expand her experience, her understanding, her personality. Phoeby replies for all black women who have never been admitted to the Doll's House."[46]

At about the age of sixteen, Janie is compelled by her grandmother, Nanny, to marry an older farmer, Logan Killicks. For Nanny the attraction of Killicks is that he owns sixty acres of land. It is important to her that Janie is economically secure and protected. Wise in the ways of the world, Nanny explains to Janie that it is necessary to have the type of security, protection, and life-style that Killicks can provide. Since Nanny is convinced that men of both races have made African-American women the "mule[s] of the world," Killicks presents a reasonable alternative. Nanny envisions a life of leisure for Janie, a life that is derived from Euro-American values and that is far from the experience of most African-American women.

Janie is very unhappy in her marriage to Killicks; she is waiting for love to appear. Love never comes, and eventually the bloom wears off the marriage for both. Killicks is no longer deferential and kind toward her. He tries to remove her from "her place" in the kitchen to work with him in the fields. The incident that convinces Janie that she is no longer loved or respected by Killicks is his decision to buy Janie a mule so that she can help him with the plowing.

Simultaneous with this decision, Jody Starks, enters Janie's life. Jody and Janie run off and marry. Janie discards her apron, the symbol of her subjugation to Killicks, along the way. Jody and Janie travel to a town in Florida similar to Eatonville, where Hurston grew up. Jody subsequently and Janie becomes "Mrs. Mayor." Jody's intent is that Janie sit on the porch perfecting an image of middle-class Euro-American women, aloof from the darker-skinned townspeople. Barbara Christian clarifies Jody's position by explaining that "the mulatta usually sits there, regal in her imitation of the white folks' ways, content that she has gotten to the peak of colored society."[47] However Janie finds her new position stultifying; she wishes to be a real person instead of a "baby doll," but Jody will not allow it. Janie learns early in her marriage that sleeping with power or being a handmaiden to power is not synonymous with having one's own. Janie becomes disillusioned with her marriage to Jody.

Jody is psychologically and physically abusive, wanting to control every aspect of Janie's life. Fearing that other men might find her hair attractive, Jody commands Janie to keep it covered. He constantly reminds her of her innate female stupidity. Jody continues the "woman" insults as he continues to make every decision. Along with his house and its furnishings and Janie is simply another of his possessions. Once Jody advises a friend that he should beat his wife for her disobedience. "As Janie realizes when she hears this exchange," Dianne Sadoff indicates, "female obedience and chatteldom are a figurative death."[48] For the first time, Janie thrusts herself into a public conversation.

The turning point in their relationship comes when Jody belittles Janie for failing to measure and to cut a piece of tobacco correctly. He tells her that as she ages, she is becoming anile. Janie insults his masculinity by comparing him to a post-menopausal woman, "robbing him of his illusion of irresistible maleness that all men cherish."[49]

Jody strikes Janie, goes to bed, and never gets up. It is only when Jody is on his deathbed that Janie tries to make him understand that life with him has been detrimental to her personal growth. It is this scene about which Darwin T. Turner writes, "Never was his conduct so cruel as to deserve the vindictive attack which Janie unleashes while he is dying."[50] Rita Dandridge, in rebuttal to Turner, offers another explanation: "Janie's bold entrance into Stark's sick room might be a symbolic gesture affirming the strength and self confidence that Starks has not completely sapped out of her."[51]

Further, Turner fails to understand that although a woman marries someone whose position gives her status and wealth, his inability to allow her to develop personally, have any control over her being, or even to speak in public constitutes psychological abuse. Janie was voiceless, allowed no expression of ideas. It was impossible for her to articulate the pain that she felt when held up to public humiliation. She is not to be blamed for her reaction; she takes advantage of the only opportunity she has had. That she is finally able to talk, to express herself while Jody is on his deathbed, is not surprising.

With Jody's death, Janie discards her turban, on the same grounds that she discarded her apron when she deserted Killicks: both are symbols of her oppression. The oppression diminishes slightly in Janie's third marriage. It is in this relationship that she has more latitude. TeaCake, a man several years younger than Janie, teaches her and encourages her to participate in male activities: playing checkers, shooting, fishing, telling stories. He cannot offer her status or wealth, only himself. Together, they leave for the Everglades, where they harvest vegetables. During a flood, TeaCake is bitten by a rabid dog from whom he contracts rabies, and Janie must shoot her husband.

Even within this marriage, Janie is physically abused. TeaCake beats her, and Janie pretends to like it or at least to tolerate it. There is no outward public reaction by Janie against this abuse. Alice Walker contends that this is the real reason that Janie kills TeaCake.

Or, rather, this is the reason Hurston *permits* Janie to kill TeaCake in the end. For all her "helpless" hanging on him Janie knows she has been publicly humiliated, and though she acts the role of battered wife . . . her developing consciousness of self does not stop at that point.[52]

In Janie Mae Crawford, Hurston creates an African-American woman who is in rebellion against male prerogative. Janie is not necessarily a character who would be a credit to her race; rather, she is a character who is a credit to her gender. Janie's race cannot be dismissed as a contributing factor to her evolution. Early in the novel Nanny warns her of the impact

that her race might have on others. To impress upon Janie the possible
repercussions of her race and gender, Nanny tells of her rape by her owner
and the subsequent actions of his wife. Nanny follows the story of her rape
with the rape of Janie's mother, reminding Janie that African-American
women have historically been sexually abused with no recourse. Along
with Nanny's descriptive historical discourse is her analysis of the ra-
cial/sexual power hierarchy as it exists in the United States.

So de white man throw down de load and tell de nigger man tuh pick it up. He
pick it up because he have to, but he don't tote it. He hand it to his womenfolks.
De nigger woman is de mule uh de world so fur as Ah can see. Ah been prayin'
fuh it tuh be different wid you. (14)

Unlike Nella Larsen, Hurston did not write about the mulatto aristocracy.
But like Larsen, Hurston fights against Janie's acceptance of the restrictions of "ladyhood," which would admit acceptance of Euro-American
standards of female behavior. Helga Crane apparently submitted to some
of the forces that determined her behavior as a woman, while Janie seems
to have won the right to self-determination and self-definition.

After the publication of Hurston's novel, Richard Wright and other male
writers became the focus of African-American writing. The impact of the
hostile urban environment became the predominant theme of the writing
of the 1940s and the 1950s. Wright's analyses of the effect of social
deprivation of African-Americans became elements of Ann Petry's first
novel, *The Street*. Although Petry writes in the naturalistic mode prevalent
in the 1940s, that element will not be considered here. Rather the focus
will be on her depiction of the female character, Lutie Johnson.

The Street, as Barbara Christian observes, functions as a "transition from
the tragic mulatta pattern and/or the rural southern woman as heroine to a
more contemporary view of the black novel."[53] The opening paragraph
portends the life that awaits Lutie Johnson and her son, Bub. Like the wind
in the opening chapter that scatters litter and people alike, Lutie's life will
be buffeted by social and cultural forces that will assault her sense of self
and dignity, never allowing her to meet her goals.

In 1944, Lutie Johnson has moved to Harlem after the failure of her
marriage. Like Janie Mae Crawford, she has been forced into an early
marriage because of the security the marriage would provide. But the
marriage fails primarily because of the inability of her husband to find
work. His constant unemployment causes Lutie to accept work as a live-in
domestic. While working for the Chandlers, she becomes imbued with

Euro-American cultural values, which emphasize the belief that success is possible if one works hard enough.

She adopts the Protestant work ethic, choosing Benjamin Franklin as her hero. Lutie accepts the American myth that Franklin, who had arrived in Philadelphia with only two loaves of bread, had prospered. Although she had learned from the Chandlers' experiences that the mere possession of money could not buy happiness, she pursues her dream.

Fighting for her dream of upward mobility, she works in a cleaner's as a presser during the day and studies typing and shorthand at night to prepare herself for a better job. After she obtains a position as a file clerk, she continues to study for promotions. Still, she is unable to save so that she and her son can move from their dingy apartment. Somehow, however, she knows that she will achieve success.

The door opens a crack when she meets Boots, a band leader, who tells her she can become a singer in his band. But Boots reneges when Junto, the Euro-American owner of the Casino Night Club, tells Boots that he wants Lutie for himself. Lutie refuses both Boots and Junto, recalling bits of conversation she had heard when working for the Chandlers. "I wouldn't have any good looking colored wench in my house. Not with John. You know they're always making passes at men. Especially white men. . . . Besides, she's colored and you know how they are—."[54]

Lutie understood perfectly this type of thinking that automatically evoked cultural stereotypes of African-American women. She knew that her race and her gender made her immediately suspect and available. Lutie's grandmother, like Janie Mae Crawford's Nanny, had frequently cautioned her of the indecent intentions of Euro-American men.

But the grandmother forgot to warn Lutie about African-American men. Certain traits are not confined to one group. Unlike society during the period of slavery or in rural Southern environments, the urban North produced little contact between Euro-American men and African-American women, and the Euro-American male was not always the enemy, as Lutie discovers. In desperate need of money and her eight-year-old son having been arrested, Lutie goes to Boots. Boots tells her that she can have the money, but she must submit to both him and Junto. Boots' slap after she spurns his sexual advances triggers the release of a lifetime of suppressed anger, violence, and frustration. Her subsequent killing of Boots is the culmination of years of disappointment. Thus, according to Gloria Wade-Gayles, she becomes the "first female protagonist in black American fiction to commit murder as an expression of her rage."[55]

Petry's stated purpose "is to show how simply and easily the environment can change the course of a person's life."[56] The environment that changes Lutie Johnson is composed of economic, sexual, and racial forces that she is unable to overcome. Lutie is defeated because she yearns for more than the options allowed African-American women within a racist-sexist system. She is very naive in her estimation of this system; she cannot comprehend that as an African-American woman she is excluded from the American dream. Although unable to change the system or to work within it, she—like many other women—blames herself for the failures in her life. Even so, Lutie never loses her dignity as a woman. The stereotypical images of African-American women held by the dominant society were never the images that she had of herself.

Lutie Johnson in a Northern urban environment succumbed to the forces that constantly assailed her, but Maude Martha in a similar environment lived a somewhat different life. *Maude Martha* is Pulitzer Prize winner (1950) Gwendolyn Brooks' (1917–) first and only novel to date.

The novel, or more properly, novella, is, as Christian contends, "a definite shift in the fiction of Afro-American women, a shift in point of view and intention that still characterizes the novels written today."[57] Maude Martha is not a Southern tragic mulatta, nor is she buffeted by social and economic forces beyond her control like Lutie Johnson. She is an ordinary woman living an ordinary life of struggle with the colorism prevalent in the African-American community, as well as with a chauvinistic husband and her "self." Brooks claims that her only intention in *Maude Martha* was "to paint a portrait of an ordinary African-American woman, first as a daughter, then as a mother and to show what she makes of her 'little life.' "[58] Maude Martha's "little life" is composed of finding beauty and pleasure in simple things, but she is also hurt, angered, and confused by incidents and events beyond her control.

The colorism found within the African-American community is a continual source of pain to Maude Martha. She recalls that as a child, she was rejected by a classmate who found her too dark. Helen, her sister, receives more love, attention, and respect from their father than Maude Martha because Helen's skin is lighter. Later, Maude Martha fears additional rejection from her husband, Paul, because of her dark color.

Maude Martha is a shy, introspective woman who reacts inwardly to the racism that she finds when she ventures outside her South Side Chicago kitchenette apartment. Whether it is the word *nigger* or trying to explain to her daughter that Santa Claus likes her, too, she is calm, patient, and outwardly accepting of the situation. Maude Martha is not an upper-class mulatta like Helga Crane, nor is she unaware of the effects of racism, sexism, and colorism that surround her as they did Lutie Johnson. She reacts carefully and intelligently to those situations that affect her. Maude

Martha is not blissfully oblivious to the societal forces that affect her. Like Lutie Mae Johnson, she is enraged, but her anger is kept under control. She never explodes in a murderous rage. Brooks has created in Maude Martha a female character who is warm, human, humble, and intelligent.

Novelist Paule Marshall has pointed to *Maude Martha* as the finest portrayal of an African-American woman in the American novel and has written of its influence on her own work.[59] Marshall's own strength, according to many literary critics, lies in her character development. Perhaps this is the influence that Brooks' *Maude Martha* has had on her writing. Brooks focuses on Maude Martha's self-exploration and her willingness to stay in touch with herself; Marshall, in *Brown Girl, Brownstones,* also creates a character who seeks to explore and develop her "self."

Paule Marshall (1929-), the daughter of West Indian immigrants, was born in Brooklyn, New York, and has spent most of her life in the New York area. She has published four books of fiction.[60] *Brown Girl, Brownstones,* which contains "poetic imagery as effective as that in Toomer's *Cane,* dialect as precise as that of Miss Hurston's *Their Eyes Were Watching God,* and the kind of gentle warmth found in Miss Brooks' *Maude Martha,*"[61] is the story of Selina Boyce from adolescence to young adulthood.

In the creation of Selina, perhaps the fictional alter-ego of Paule Marshall, another aspect of the African-American experience is added, that of the immigrant, which is unique in African-American writing. As West Indian immigrants, the Boyces cannot become part of the Euro-American social fabric, and they are not sure they can be or want to become part of the African-American tradition.

Although the novel centers around Selina, her mother, Silla, becomes the more interesting character. In the portrayal of the two female characters, it is possible for all the stereotypes of African-American women to come into play. However, as the reader comes to know Silla and her "kitchen" compatriots, stereotypical images are put to rest.

Marshall insists that she is not portraying a matriarchy; rather, by using a female environment, the kitchen, she allows her characters to explore and recreate their lives. The women who sit in the kitchen and "talk" their lives have their own authority, their own sense of self, and their own strengths—not a particular kind of strength that has been assigned to them by a racist-sexist society but their personally developed strengths, which help them to survive. Yet, for all their strength, authority, and sense of self, they are no less female. Silla is one of these women.

Silla seems to be a confused woman, but her confusion is a typically American confusion or even an immigrant confusion. Like Lutie Johnson, she has adopted the American dream. Silla has come to the United States to take advantage of the available economic opportunities and becomes imbued with the notion of success. For her, the American dream will be achieved through the acquisition of property. This rush to obtain real estate clouds her judgment and her vision, causing her to destroy her marriage and alienate her children. Still, unlike Lutie Mae Johnson, Silla recognizes the limitations that society has placed on her race and gender and works within those parameters. The novel ends with Silla's husband's committing suicide after his deportation, in which Silla played a significant part. Selena, Silla's daughter, then goes to the West Indies to discover her roots, and, consequently, herself.

A matured, middle-aged Selena can possibly be found in Marshall's short story "Reena" (1962), one of the "first pieces of Afro-American fiction to delve into the complex choices confronting the contemporary, educated Black woman."[62] Reena, like Maude Martha, is self-exploratory; she knows what she wants from life. As a woman who has fought her way from working-class to middle-class status, she has had experiences that are similar to those of other African-American women: rejection by African-American men, single parenthood, underemployment, and awareness of their images as women.

That definition of me . . . formulated by others to serve out their fantasies, a definition we have to combat at an unconscionable cost to the self and even use, at times, in order to survive; the cause of so much shame and rage as well as, oddly enough, a source of pride: simply what it has meant, what it means, to be a Black woman in America.[63]

Reena, like Maude Martha, has been subjected to colorism through rejection by her light-skinned boyfriend's parents, to whom she was not a person but rather "a symbol of the darkness they were in flight from."[64] Like many other African-American women during the turbulent 1960s, she has participated in radical politics and taken a Euro-American lover. She eventually marries her lover and begins the life of the typical American housewife, but the husband's career as a photographer is not successful, and more and more he takes out his frustrations on her. There is a divorce, and she is left to raise her children alone. Reena blames many of her marital problems on her absent husband and, in a sense, blames all African-American men for the problems of African-American women.

After the divorce, however, Reena's sense of independence emerges, and she begins to plan a husbandless, fatherless life for herself and her children, a life that includes possibly living and working in Africa. She tells her friend that she has everything she needs: her children and her career. Having suffered the constraints of an American marriage, she feels that she must live her life alone. But neither she nor her friend will spare themselves the brutal truth that they feel rejected by African-American men.

In her fiction Marshall explores the racism that permeates American society, but the racism gives way to the sexism of the African-American community. Marshall's characters strive to avoid the racism and sexism in Western societies by journeying to other places. Selena goes to the West Indies, Reena and Merle Kimbona (*The Chosen Place, The Timeless People*) to Africa, and Avey Johnson (*Praisesong for the Widow*) to Tatum Island. They leave the United States in search of a place to find themselves rather than looking inside for the answers they seek. Toni Morrison, on the other hand, creates a character, Sula Mae Peace, who returns to the place of her origin to find her answers.

Chloe Anthony "Toni" Morrison (1929-), the author of six works of fiction,[65] was born in Lorain, Ohio. She received the 1978 National Book Critics Circle Award for Fiction for *Song of Solomon* and in 1988 won the Pulitzer Prize for fiction with *Beloved*. Morrison is a senior editor at Random House. In Sula, Morrison "created the most radical of characters . . . [one who] overturns the conventional definition of good and evil in relation to women by insisting that she exists primarily as and for herself—not to be a mother or to be a lover of men."[66]

Sula is one of the Peace women (Eva, Hannah, and Sula) who lived in the small town of Medallion, Ohio, from 1920 to 1965. *Sula* is the intriguing story of an enigmatic, headstrong woman whose unorthodox behavior confounds the townspeople. As an adolescent Sula exhibits some of the behavior that will be seen in her adult life. When she and her friend, Nel, are accosted by young Irish toughs, Sula calmly and deliberately cuts off the tip of her finger. Sula's act not only apprises the boys of their own vulnerability when confronted by a provoked, determined African-American woman, but it also confirms that she will not be dominated by Euro-American men.

Sula grows up in a female-headed household with her mother, Hannah, and her grandmother, Eva. Each is responsible for shaping Sula's personality and her sense of reality. Eva was deserted by her husband Boy-Boy (twice immature) and left with three children, five eggs, and three beets. She left Medallion and returned eighteen months later with one leg missing and a monthly insurance check. The village gossip was that she had deliberately allowed a train to sever the leg.

Even with her hatred and mistrust of Boy-Boy, Eva fervently believed that women should cater to men, and she had bequeathed this love of men to her daughters. Hannah's husband had died when Sula was three years old, and they returned to lived with Eva. Hannah is a completely free sexual being who gives herself willingly despite a lack of masculine commitment. In forming her "self," Sula decides that she need not be like her mother or grandmother.

The third woman who influences Sula is Nel, with whom she had formed a friendship when they were both twelve years old. Separately yet simultaneously, they had discovered that "they were neither white nor male, and that all freedom and triumph was forbidden to them, they had set about creating something else to be."[67]

Nel is not as creative as Sula. She eventually accepts the cultural assumptions about a "woman's place" because she had acquiesced to her mother's opinions, whereas Sula, for much of her life, uncategorically rejects the community's rigid standards for women. Because Sula rejected patriarchal standards for the behavior of women, she could leave Medallion after Nel's marriage. Ten years later, she returns, accompanied by a plague of robins. She finds that Nel has become a wife like all the other married women in the community, who were in a restrictive moribund condition. Morrison parallels women writers before and after her who equate marriage with death. Sula immediately shocks the community with her contempt for their traditions. She uses the village men as sexual objects in the same manner as her mother had used them. But she does not cater to them, nor does she domesticate herself for them.

The village women become hostile to her. Sula flaunts all of their traditions and values. And the women, perhaps out of spiteful jealousy, become more virulent in their hatred of her. Sula did not age, she did not gain weight, she had all of her teeth, and this contributed to the continued antagonism that the village women had for her. But it is the village men who damn her in the community; they accuse her of sleeping with Euro-American men. This act is somehow more immoral than sleeping with Afro-American men. Sula was being accused of lacking both knowledge of her history and racial pride.

Sula has little sympathy for the particular pains of African-American men within a racist society. After all, according to Sula, African-American men are much better off than African-American women. They are not subjected to the sexism that permeates American society; rather they are among the primary supporters of sexism and oppressors of women. Sula rejects the African-American males' criticism of Euro-American society by forcing Nel's husband, Jude, to confront directly the privileges that he enjoys as a male. At the same time, she rejects society's traditional roles for women, particularly those concerning motherhood. Sula's rejection of these roles, her relationship with men, and her love for Nel cause Barbara Smith [68] to interpret Sula's behavior as latent lesbianism. While Smith's argument seems logical and cogent, it does not stand up to close scrutiny. In an interview,[69] Morrison emphatically denies the possibility of a homosexual relationship between Nel and Sula.

Sula is sexually free and uninhibited, as was her mother, Hannah. Unlike her mother, Sula uses men in the same manner that they would use her. Nel, her alter-ego, has opted to be the "hem—the tuck and fold that hid his [Jude's] raveling edges; a someone, sweet, industrious and loyal to shore him up."[70] In short, Nel has embraced all the qualities and characteristics usually assigned to the "good" woman.

Sula, on the other hand, decides that she can have it all despite Nel's exasperation.

You *can't* do it all. You a woman and a colored woman at that. You can't act like a man. You can't be walking around all independent-like, doing whatever you like, taking what you can't, leaving what you don't.
    . . . You say I'm a woman and colored. Ain't that the same as being a man?[71]

Maxine Hong Kingston has expressed approximately the same viewpoint in *The Woman Warrior.* "Isn't a bad girl almost a boy?"[72] the narrator asks. Ultimately, Sula is labeled "bad" because the male definition of female "badness" is accepted by both men and female supporters of men. Sula therefore becomes bad by masculine standards because she lives, thinks, and behaves as men do.

Sula had confronted her society's assumptions concerning the position and role of women, rightly assuming that women had options other than wife and mother. But in doing so, she had also challenged the right of men to define female roles. In a sense she had shattered some of the illusions of male privilege. When a woman deviates from the decrees of the patriarchy, she must be punished, ostracized, or die—all of which happened to Sula.

In the 1970s and 1980s African-American women writers began to question the assumption of male superiority. Genital politics, which advocates male superiority, was being rejected for the right of women to assert themselves in areas where they had once been denied. In a *New York Times*

Book Review article entitled "Sexism, Racism and Black Women Writers,"
Mel Watkins lambasted those African-American women writers

who have chosen black men as a target [and] have set themselves outside a
tradition that is nearly as old as black American literature itself. They have, in
effect, put themselves at odds with what seems to be an unspoken but almost
universally accepted covenant among black writers.[73]

The "universally accepted covenant" of which Watkins writes is that
African-American literature concentrate on rectifying the images created
by non-African-American writers. Therefore, negative images of African-
American men and women should not be presented in fiction by African-
American writers, but women, in particular, should not depict negative
male characters. Watkins harks back to an earlier time when W. E. B. Du
Bois exhorted African-American writers to produce only humane, positive
images of African-Americans, not necessarily realistic images. To this
suggestion Langston Hughes replied,

We younger Negro artists who create now intend to express our dark-skinned
selves without fear or shame. If white people are pleased, we are glad. If they are
not, it doesn't matter. . . . If colored people are pleased, we are glad. If they are
not, their displeasure doesn't matter either.[74]

However, it seems that Watkins has forgotten the words of Hughes or
is unfamiliar with them. Some African-American male writers have
embellished those stereotypes of African-American women in their writing without an uproar from the community. It seems that it is appropriate
for men to disparage women but not vice-versa. One of the women writers
who became embroiled in this controversy was Alice Walker, who has
been criticized for her depiction of men (Mister, Harpo, etc.) in her Pulitzer
Prize–winning novel (1982) *The Color Purple*.

Alice Walker (1944-) was born in Eatonton, Georgia. She is a prolific
writer, having published three volumes of poetry, a collection of essays,
two collections of short stories, and four novels.[75] An analysis of these
writings reveals her concern for the lives of African-American women.
Walker has stated that she is "committed to exploring the oppressions, the
insanities, the loyalties, and the triumphs of black women, . . . the most
fascinating creations in the world."[76] She presents some of these fascinating creations in her collection of short stories, *In Love and Trouble*.

Walker has described the women of these stories and some of her other
fiction as "suspended." In defining "suspended," Walker borrows Zora
Neale Hurston's term, "mules of the world." Walker uses this image

because "we [African-American women] have been handed the burdens that everyone else—*everyone* else—refused to carry."[77]

Walker's women are "creatures so abused and mutilated in body, so dimmed and confused by pain that they considered themselves unworthy even of hope."[78] But somehow they developed "contrary instincts," the insistence on challenging convention, on being themselves, sometimes in spite of themselves, and the courage to fight back, if only in their thoughts. The women of *In Love and Trouble* dream and develop "contrary instincts."

The collection opens with two excerpts, the first from Elechi Amadi's *The Concubine* and the second from Rainer Maria Rilke's *Letters to a Young Poet*. Amadi's Ahurole had normally been a cheerful, happy young woman, but for the past year she had been depressed, crying, and sorrowful. No one knew why. Her parents believed that "she was being unduly influence by *agwu*, her personal spirit." At the end of the excerpt, the reader learns that "Ahurole was engaged to Ekwuene when she was eight days old." She was depressed by her loss of personal autonomy, which her society's traditions had eliminated.

In the second excerpt, Walker uses Rilke to explain that "we must hold to what is difficult, everything in Nature grows and defends itself . . . and is characteristically and spontaneously itself, seeks at all costs to be so and against all opposition."[79] The short stories of *In Love and Trouble* follow Rilke's philosophy.

In "Roselily," the opening story, Roselily believes the difficult thing to do is the right thing. She is being married because it is expected of her. It is her wedding day, a day of celebration and triumphant delivery from the poverty and hard work that she has experienced all her life. Instead, Roselily, who is marrying a Muslim, looks forward to her new life with foreboding, although it is a life that will give her what she wants most: respect. However, she understands the restrictions that the new religion will place on her as a woman. But to her, the mother of four illegitimate children, marriage should be liberating. Marriage will bring Roselily financial security; she will no longer work outside her home. But she also realizes that marriage is another form of imprisonment.

Roselily can express her aversion to her own situation only in her thoughts during the ceremony. Similar to Ahurole, Roselily is trapped by tradition and cannot or will not resist that tradition. Walker uses images that evoke oppression: quicksand, flowers choked to death, ropes, chains, handcuffs, cemeteries, a cornered rat. Mary Helen Washington comments that the "very robe and veil she is wearing are emblems of servitude that she yearns to be free of."[80]

In contrast to Roselily, Myrna, the protagonist of "Really, Doesn't Crime Pay?" is the wife of a successful Southern African-American man. Still, she too is trapped by her husband's and society's view of women. Although her confinement is not behind a veil, as Roselily's will be, Myrna's confinement is in the mythology of Southern womanhood. However, unlike Roselily, Myrna does more than dream; she writes. In a series of journal entries, she tells how the restrictions imposed upon her by her husband stifle her creativity.

Myrna knows that her value is in her appearance and social position, not in her creativity. Nevertheless, Myrna wants Ruel, her husband, to understand that she is not only a womb and that she needs more than afternoons at the local shopping center to be a complete person. In frustration, she attempts to murder her husband with a chain saw. This act is viewed in society as madness rather than frustration over a situation in which she is powerless. Myrna is committed to an asylum. After a year, Myrna returns, determined to kill Ruel, this time with "yes." That is, like a good wife, she will be promptly and methodically compliant.

The young female protagonists in the volume struggle against society's imposed conventions through dreaming and writing. In contrast, the older women act; they are survivors. Hannah Hemhuff in "The Revenge of Hannah Hemhuff" feels that she must relieve her suffering and at the same time exact revenge.

During the depression, Hannah and her family are starving. She dresses herself, her husband, and her children in clothing sent "from up North" and goes to the bread line. Not only is she refused food by that "little slip of a woman," but her husband abandons her for another woman in the same line. Eventually her children die of starvation, and Hannah is forced into prostitution.

After many years, Hannah visits Tante Rosie, the local root worker (one who uses roots and herbs for medicinal purposes or for charms and spells), in order to exact revenge on the "little white moppet" who had caused her so much pain. Hannah dies soon after her visit to Tante Rosie, but within months the "little white moppet" is also dead. Hannah had acted using the most common tool available to Southern African-American women, conjure.

Not only had Hannah acted, but so did the lady of "The Welcome Table." The old lady had the audacity to enter a Euro-American church to worship. The male ushers were unsure of how to handle the situation, but unsurprisingly the women knew exactly what to do: throw her out. Walker censures not only Euro-American Christianity but also Euro-American women. While standing on the steps after being ejected from the church, the old lady sees Jesus. She and Jesus walk and talk for a long time. The old lady's body is later found on the highway; people assumed she had walked herself to death. Walker implies that the old lady, like Enoch, had walked with God and ascended to heaven.

The stories in *In Love and Trouble* are provocative, clearly demonstrating Walker's stated purpose of presenting the "contrary instincts" of African-American women. Possessing these instincts, Walker's female characters do not care how others see them. Their concern is with being true to themselves. It seems that in the development of these characters, work by African-American women writers that is intended to refute negative images and "uplift" the race might be at an end.

Overall, these women write about African-American women—their hopes, fears, experiences, history, and images. They promote the importance of female friendships: Linda Brent and her grandmother, Sappho and Dora, Helga and Mrs. Hayes-Rore, Janie and Phoeby, Nel and Sula.

With the practicality of female friendship is the important element of paid employment. Frado has to work for her survival, eventually turning to writing in an effort to save her child; Iola Leroy, Sappho Clark, Helga Crane, Lutie Mae Johnson, Maude Martha, Selena, and Nel work at some point in their lives. These women characters frequently work because of their very definite ideas about the institution of marriage, usually equating it with imprisonment or death. If marriage is not always a part of their lives, neither are men who are absent, through either desertion or divorce. African-American men are usually portrayed as wishing to emulate patriarchal authority without the financial means, cultural knowledge, or Euro-American masculine privilege. After they discover that they do not have this privilege, they abandon or exploit African-American women, the only exploitable people available to them.

As perhaps an answer to the accusation of African-American female immorality, Larsen and Morrison underscore female sexuality by showing how their characters grapple with and attempt to resolve the issue. Larsen's Helga Crane battles her sexual self to disprove theories of African-American female sexuality, only to succumb to a man whom earlier she would have found distasteful. Morrison's Sula ignores conventions and pursues her personal ideas of what a woman can and should be, only to be destroyed by village gossip, disease, and the loss of her best friend. Both authors imply that society is male structured and that women who defy the structure are doomed.

There are mulattas, mothers and women who could be perceived as "loose," but these traits are presented as individual qualities rather than racial traits. These women writers do not merely strive to create "positive" images of the African-American woman—representations that often contradicted reality. They have instead chosen to challenge those inaccurate images through the creation of more well-defined characters. These African-American women writers are conceiving new African-American female characters who confront their history and the distortion of their ethnicity and gender that have arisen from the racism, sexism, and classism prevalent in American society.

NOTES

1. Gloria Wade-Gayles, *No Crystal Stair. Visions of Race and Sex in Black Women's Fiction* (New York: Pilgrim Press, 1984), 7.

2. Ann Allen Shockley, *Afro-American Women Writers: 1746–1933* (New York: New American Library, 1988), 19.

3. Richard Wright, "The Literature of the Negro of the United States," in *White Man Listen!* (Garden City, NY: Doubleday and Company, 1964), 76.

4. Many references to Africa are found in *The Poems of Phillis Wheatley*, ed. Julian D. Mason (Chapel Hill: The University of North Carolina Press, 1989). Some examples are: "To Maecenas," "On Virtue," "On the Death of the Reverend Mr. George Whitefield, 1770," "On Recollection," "To the Right Honorable William, Earl of Dartmouth, His Majesty's Principle Secretary of State for North-America," "A Elegiac Poem on the Death of George Whitefield," "An Ode of Verses on the Death of George Whitefield," "Deism," "An Address to the Deist," "America," "The Answer," "Phillis's Reply to the Answer," "On the Death of General Wooster."

5. Shockley, 19

6. Richard Long and Eugenia W. Collier, eds., *Afro-American Writing. An Anthology of Prose and Poetry* (University Park, PA: The Pennsylvania University Press, 1985), 13.

7. Alice Walker, *In Search of Our Mother's Gardens* (New York: Harcourt Brace Jovanovich, 1983), 237.

8. Ann Plato, *Essays, Including Biographies and Miscellaneous Pieces in Prose and Poetry*, 1841; Zilpha Elaw, *Memoirs of the Life, Religious Experience, Ministerial Travels and Labours, of Mrs. Zilpha, an American Female of Colour; Together with Some Account of the Great Religious Revivals in America*, 1846; Jarena Lee, *Religious Experience and Journal of Jarena Lee, Giving an Account of Her Call to Preach the Gospel*, 1849; Nancy Gardener Prince, *A Narrative of the Life and Travels of Mrs. Nancy Prince*, 1850.

9. Henry Louis Gates lists Maria F. dos Reis, *Ursula*, in Brazil in 1859 as the second woman in the introduction to *Our Nig; or, Sketches from the Life of a*

Free Black, In a Two-Story House, North. Showing That Slavery's Shadows Fall Even There by Harriet E. Wilson, with introduction and notes by Henry Louis Gates, Jr. (New York: Random House, Vintage Books, 1983), xiii.

10. Ibid., xxviii.

11. Ibid., xxvi, xxix.

12. Shockley, 86.

13. Estelle C. Jelinek, *The Tradition of Women's Biographies: From Antiquity to the Present* (Boston: Twayne Publishers, 1986), 79.

14. Harriet A. Jacobs, *Incidents in the Life of a Slave Girl. Written by Herself* (Cambridge: Harvard University Press, 1987 [1861]), 77.

15. Ibid., 54–55.

16. Lerone Bennet, *Before the Mayflower: A History of the Negro in America, 1619–1964* (Baltimore: Penguin Books, 1966), 235–36, 280.

17. Ida B. Wells-Barnett, *On Lynchings* (New York: Arno Press and The New York Times, 1969), 4.

18. Alice Walker defines womanist as "from *womanish*. . . . A black feminist or feminist of color. . . . Usually referring to outrageous, audacious, courageous or *willful* behavior. . . . A woman who. . . . appreciates and prefers women's culture. . . . woman is to feminist as purple is to lavender."

19. Carole McAlpine Watson, *Prologue. The Novels of Black American Women, 1891–1965* (Westport, CT: Greenwood Press, 1985), 12.

20. Amelia Etta Hall Johnson's *Clarence and Corinne; or God's Way* (1890) and Emma Dunham Kelly's *Megda* (1891) predate Frances Harper's *Iola Leroy*.

21. Harper wrote the first short story by an African-American woman, "The Two Offers," which was published in the *Anglo-American* for September and October 1859, and ten volumes of poetry.

22. This point was reinforced in publications of the period such as *Reedy's Mirror*, published in St. Louis, MO, which in the September 11, 1902, issue quoted an English social critic, Gerard Mansel, who advocated "laws making it illegal for women to earn their own livelihood [because] it endangers the vitality and progress of civilized nations."

23. Frances E. W. Harper, *Iola Leroy or Shadows Uplifted* (Boston: Beacon Press, 1987 [1893]), 210.

24. Anna Julia Cooper, *A Voice from the South.* (New York: Oxford University Press, 1988 [1892]), 68.

25. Barbara Christian, *Black Women Novelists. The Development of a Tradition, 1892–1976* (Westport, CT: Greenwood Press, 1980), 5.

26. *Clarence and Corinne; or, God's Way*, 1890; *The Hazeley Family*; *Martina Meriden; or, What Is My Motive*, 1901.

27. (Pseudonym, Sarah A. Allen) *Hagar's Daughters, a Story of Southern Caste Prejudice*, 1902; *Of One Blood; or the Hidden Self*, 1902–3; *A Primer of Facts Pertaining to the Early Greatness of the African Race and the Possibility of Restoration by Its Decendants—with Epilogue*, 1905.

28. The magazine stated that she had resigned because of ill health.

29. Pauline Hopkins, *Contending Forces: A Romance Illustrative of Negro Life North and South* (Boston: Colored Co-Operative Publishing Co., 1900), 13–14.

30. Ibid., 125.

31. Different scholars have established different dates for the beginning and ending of the movement. Some scholars date the movement as early as 1903 with the publication of Du Bois' *The Souls of Black Folks* or as late as 1925 with the publication of Alain Locke's *The New Negro*.

32. John Hope Franklin, *From Slavery to Freedom: A History of Negro Americans,* Fifth Edition (New York: Alfred A. Knopf, 1980), 362.

33. *There Is Confusion,* 1924; *Plum Bun: A Novel without a Moral,* 1929; *The Chinaberry Tree: A Novel of American Life,* 1931; *Comedy, American Style,* 1933.

34. *The Heart of a Woman and Other Poems,* 1918; *Bronze: A Book of Verse,* 1923; *An Autumn Love Cycle,* 1928.

35. *Songs from the Wayside,* 1908; *A Garland of Poems,* 1926.

36. *Fifty Years of Freedom; or From Cabin to Congress, a Drama in Five Acts,* 1910.

37. *Fool's Errand: A Play in One Act,* 1927.

38. Langston Hughes, "The Negro Artist and the Racial Mountain," *The Nation* (June 23, 1926): 692–93.

39. Nella Larsen, *Quicksand* (Brunswick, NJ: Rutgers University Press, 1986 [1928]), 7.

40. Ibid., 12.

41. Deborah McDowell, introduction to *Quicksand,* xix.

42. To many early Americans, black skin and the word *slave* were synonymous. With miscegenation and concomitantly increasing laws that attempted to define "black," the problems became more pressing. The concept of *partus sequitur ventrem* had been in effect since the seventeenth century, making slavery a condition of birth as well as color. To strengthen the equation of blackness and slavery, many states began to set down "exact" definitions of blackness. Georgia defined Black as negroes [*sic*], mulattoes, mestizos and their descendants having any ascertainable trace of either negro [*sic*] or African, West Indian or Asiatic Indian blood. Louisiana defines an African-American as all persons with any appreciable mixture of Negro blood. In 1819, the South Carolina courts defined a Negro as a slave, or subject to becoming a slave, and that a slave was *ipso facto* a Negro. The Mississippi Supreme Court said that in the eyes of the law a Negro is *prima facie* a slave.

Although *mulatto* was the word most commonly used to indicate a person of mixed blood, many other sociological, if not biological, terms were developed to ensure that any person with a visible mixture of white "blood" would be recognized as African. Edward B. Reuters in *The Mulatto in the United States* (New York: Johnson Reprint collection, 1970, 1918) (p. 13) gives the following general categories:

mulatto	Negro and white
quadroon	mulatto and white
octoroon	quadroon and white
mustifie	octoroon and white
mustifino	mustifie and white

In 1856 Louisiana introduced the following classifications of African-Americans:

sacatra	griffe and negress [*sic*]
griffe	Negro and mulatto
marabon	mulatto and griffe
mulatto	white and Negro
quadroon	white and mulatto
metif	white and quadroon
meamelouc	white and metif
quarteron	white and meamelous
sang-mele	white and quarteron

Archy Moore (*Archy Moore, the White Slave or Memoirs of a Fugitive*) and Clotelle (*Clotelle*) could have been octoroon, mustifie, or mustifino, although Helga Crane (*Quicksand*) was undoubtedly mulatta. Who is or is not of African descent was not a problem confined to the nineteenth century. The United States Bureau of the Census declares: "A person of mixed white and Negro blood should be returned as a Negro, no matter how small the percentage [the infamous one drop] of Negro blood. Black and mulatto persons are to be returned as Negroes, without distinction. . . . Mixtures of nonwhite races should be reported according to the race of the father, except that Negro-Indian should be reported as Indian" [*The Negro Yearbook* (New York: William H. Wise and Co., Inc., 1952), 1].

In 1978 Susie Guillory Phipps of Sulphur, Louisiana, began a lawsuit against the state of Louisiana seeking to change her racial designation. Mrs. Phipps had lived her entire life as a Euro-American, although she was classified as "colored" on her birth certificate. Under a previous law repealed in 1983, Louisiana classified anyone with 1/32 African ancestry as Black. In 1987 the United States Supreme Court declined to hear her case.

43. McDowell, xxi.

44. Hortense Thornton, "Sexism as Quagmire: Nella Larsen's *Quicksand*," *CLA Journal* 16 (March 1973): 288, 291.

45. *Jonah's Gourd Vine*, 1934; *Mules and Men*, 1935; *Their Eyes Were Watching God*, 1937; *Tell My Horse*, 1938; *Moses, Man of the Mountain*, 1939; *Dust Tracks on a Road*, 1942; *Seraph on the Suwanee*, 1948.

46. Jay Walker, "Zora Neale Hurston's *Their Eyes Were Watching God*: Black Novel of Sexism," *Modern Fiction Studies* 20 (1974): 362.

47. Barbara Christian, *Black Feminist Criticism. Perspectives on Black Women Writers* (New York: Pergamon Press, 1985), 37.

48. Dianne F. Sadoff, "Black Matrilineage: The Case of Alice Walker and Zora Neale Hurston," *Signs: Journal of Women in Society* 2 (Autumn 1985): 17.

49. Zora Neale Hurston, *Their Eyes Were Watching God* (Urbana: University of Illinois Press, 1978 [1937]), 121.

50. Darwin T. Turner, *In a Minor Chord. Three Afro-American Writers and Their Search for Identity.* (Carbondale: Southern Illinois University Press, 1971), 108.

51. Rita B. Dandridge, "Male Critics/Black Women's Novels," *CLA Journal* 22(September 1979): 8, 9.

52. Walker, 305.

53. Christian, 11.

54. Ann Petry, *The Street* (Boston: Beacon Press, 1974 [1946]), 41, 45.

55. Wade-Gayles, 148.

56. James W. Ivey, "Ann Petry Talks about Her First Novel," in *Sturdy Black Bridges. Visions of Black Women in Literature,* Roseann P. Bell, Bettye J. Parker, and Beverly Guy-Sheftall, eds. (Garden City, NY: Anchor Press, 1979), 199.

57. Barbara Christian, "Trajectories of Self-Definition: Placing Contemporary Afro-American Women's Fiction," in *Conjuring. Black Women, Fiction, and Literary Tradition*, Marjorie Pryse and Hortense J. Spillers, eds. (Bloomington: Indiana University Press, 1985), 237.

58. Ibid., 238.

59. Ibid.

60. *Soul Clap Hands and Sing,* 1961; *The Chosen Place, the Timeless People,* 1969; *Praisesong for the Widow,* 1983; *Reena and Other Stories,* 1983.

61. Roger Whitlow, *Black American Literature* (Chicago: Nelson-Hall, 1973), 139.

62. Christian, 110.

63. Paule Marshall, "Reena," in *Reena and Other Stories* (Old Westbury, NY: The Feminist Press, 1983), 73.

64. Ibid., 79.

65. *The Bluest Eye,* 1970; *Sula,* 1973; *The Song of Solomon,* 1977; *TarBaby,* 1981; *Beloved,* 1988; *Jazz,* 1992.

66. Christian, in *Conjuring*, 241.

67. Toni Morrison, *Sula* (New York: Alfred A. Knopf, 1973), 30.

68. Barbara Smith, "Toward a Black Feminist Criticism," in *But Some of Us Are Brave*, Gloria T. Hull et al., eds. (Old Westbury, NY: The Feminist Press, 1982), 157–75.

69. Claudia Tate, "An Interview with Toni Morrison," in *Black Women Writers at Work* (New York: Continuum, 1983), 118.

70. Morrison, 83.

71. Ibid., 142.

72. Maxine Hong Kingston, *The Woman Warrior. Memoirs of a Girlhood among Ghosts* (New York: Vintage Books, 1977), 54.

73. Mel Watkins, "Sexism, Racism and Black Women Writers," *New York Times Book Review* (June 15, 1986): 36.

74. Langston Hughes, "The Negro Artist and the Racial Mountain," *Nation* (June 23, 1926); 693.

75. *Once,* 1970; *Revolutionary Petunias and Other Poems,* 1973; *Goodnight Willie Lee, I'll See You in the Morning,* 1979; *In Search of Our Mother's Gardens,* 1983; *In Love and Trouble,* 1973; *You Can't Keep a Good Woman Down,* 1981; *The Third Life of Grange Copeland,* 1970; *The Color Purple,* 1982; *The Temple of My Familiar,* 1988; *Possessing the Secret of Joy,* 1992.

76. John O'Brien, ed., *Interviews with Black Women Writers* (New York: Liverwright, 1973), 192.

77. Walker, *In Search of Our Mother's Gardens* (New York: Harcourt Brace Jovanovich, 1983), 232.

78. Ibid., 237.

79. Ibid.

80. Mary Helen Washington, "An Essay on Alice Walker," in *Sturdy Black Bridges,* 140.

Chapter Four

Dragon Ladies, Susie Wongs, and Passive Dolls

African-American women writers recorded their responses to the popular images that circumscribed and distorted their existence. The stereotypes were created by Euro-American writers and were frequently supported by African-American male writers. Chinese-American women have faced a similar situation: inaccurate images created by the dominant society. These representations, like those of African-American women, were not present in the early literature of the United States but developed much later.

Historian Shih-shan Henry Tsai dates the arrival of the first Chinese in the United States as 1758 in Baltimore.[1] In succeeding years a few Chinese entered ports on the East Coast, mainly as skilled tradesmen and servants. Others eventually entered the country and settled primarily on the West Coast. As immigrants had before them, the Chinese came to the "Gold Mountain" seeking a way of life different from and better than the one that they had had in China. Most of these early Chinese in the United States can trace their roots to a small region in Guangdong Province in southern China.

During the nineteenth century Guangdong province experienced tremendous problems: overpopulation, floods, famine, land concentrated in the hands of a few wealthy landlords, domestic revolts, and the Taiping rebellion.[2] These problems caused many Chinese to emigrate under penalty of death. Upon arrival in the United States, these early immigrants found problems of a different kind awaiting them. Unfortunately, the image of disease-ridden, opium-using heathens preceded them.

These images were essentially shaped by three groups: traders, diplomats, and missionaries. In the nineteenth century these three groups were the primary sources of information disseminated in the United States about China and the Chinese. Reports by traders and diplomats were not readily available to the vast majority of the American reading public, but those of the missionaries were. In their newsletters and personal correspondence, these missionaries interpreted China and Chinese culture from an ethnocentric perspective. They never truly understood the Chinese, yet they influenced the attitudes of generations of Americans.

While they shaped many of the negative images of the Chinese, the missionaries were also responsible for promoting Chinese immigration to this country. As Stuart Miller notes in *The Unwelcome Immigrant*, as "Christianity was not gaining a foothold [in China], immigration was proposed . . . to hasten conversion."[3] In their encouragement of immigration, the missionaries hoped that the Chinese would become Christianized and return to China as missionaries themselves.

But it was the Opium War that helped popularize the most negative image of China during the middle part of the nineteenth century. The Opium War, or the first Anglo-Chinese War, was fought from 1839 to 1842. Opium had been introduced into China from India by English merchants to support their mercantile interests. The use of opium not only drained gold and silver from the country but also debased and weakened the people. The Chinese emperor, when pressed by the British to legalize the trade, refused, thus leading to the infamous war in which China suffered its first defeat at the hands of a European power. The defeat led to the Chinese becoming associated in American minds with the use of opium.

The negative images of drug-using, disease-carrying heathens were firmly in place by 1850; however, no single event or group can be held responsible. According to Miller, new critical themes had developed in the United States, especially on the West Coast: the Chinese, it was believed, espoused a different and inferior style of life; the Chinese encroached on jobs normally held by Euro-Americans; the Chinese could not or would not preserve or replicate American social order and institutions; they did not desire to become citizens;[4] they made no effort to learn the language; in short, they were unassimilable. They were seen as sojourners, that is, a people who migrated to earn money, principally building the railroads, and who then returned to China to live in their ancestral villages.[5]

Recent scholarship by Chinese-American historians such as Franklin Ng has questioned the validity of the hypothesis of the Chinese as sojourners distinct from European immigrants.[6] Ng argues that some European immigrants were also sojourners, a determination at which he arrived by examining entering and departing immigration records. But the

European immigrants were not stigmatized for their eagerness to come to the United States, earn money, and return to their native lands.

Along with the image of the Chinese as sojourners and their belief that the Chinese were unable to assimilate, some Americans also feared the Chinese association with loathsome contagious diseases such as syphilis and leprosy. Consequently, in 1882 the Congress of the United States, after much pressure from labor groups and the news media, passed the first of three Chinese Exclusion Acts. With a weak and disinterested Chinese government unwilling to defend the rights of its citizens abroad, specifically in the United States, the Chinese became fair game for racists.

However, in response to the Exclusion Act, Chinese who had lived in the United States and had returned to China began a boycott of American goods. *The Bitter Society*, written by Ku Shehui and published in Shanghai in 1905, records the sufferings of the Chinese in the United States and the necessity for retaliatory action.

The work's main theme is the discrimination against the Chinese in the United States and the need for reprisals. Its plot, however, is more comprehensive than the maltreatment of the Chinese. It traces the experiences of five indigent but educated men from China to Peru and, later, to the United States. As is pointed out, *The Bitter Society* is more a tale of Chinese emigration than a tale about the Chinese in the United States.[7]

The author gives many details about life in the United States to reinforce the call for a Chinese boycott against United States manufactured goods. Some of these details are the stoning of new Chinese arrivals in San Francisco, the incarceration of immigrants in wooden barracks (described later as cages), arbitrary arrests, and constant harassment. These are essential elements of the story, but the value lies in the descriptions of the thoughts, attitudes, and reactions of the Chinese to the discrimination. Although the boycott had little effect on Sino-American relations, it did provide information to the Chinese about life awaiting them in the United States.

The continued excesses of the press, pressures from Dennis Kearney[8] and his Nativist Party (which opposed Chinese labor), and caricatures of Asians in pulp fiction helped to promote and maintain an image of the Chinese and Chinatowns that was further embellished by some of the leading fiction writers of the time. Although the Chinese had eyes with epicanthic folds, wore queues, spoke a strange language, and followed ancient, "uncivilized" customs, they were industrious—no one denied that—but they were also depicted as cunning, cruel, inscrutable, and generally inhuman. They could never be assimilated, it was supposed, because they retained their loyalty to the Emperor, to their ancestors, and to Confucius. They had filthy social habits, lured American boys and girls into their opium dens, and plotted to take control of the Pacific Coast. Their very presence was a threat to the American way of life.

These images referred mainly to men but could be applied to women as well. The women, in addition to the basic ethnic stereotypes, had to cope with gender-specific stereotypes as well: unstinting evil, smoldering sexuality, and abject subservience.[9] Therefore, the primary images of Chinese women in the United States were the Dragon Lady, the prostitute, and the passive doll.

Before 1880 only a few Chinese women came to the United States because Chinese tradition held that no respectable woman would leave home even to accompany her husband. However, Chinese women were present in this country as early as 1834. Afong Moy[10] was reportedly the first to arrive. She was displayed in New York in an exposition that purported to authenticate the appearances of women from different parts of the world. She was followed by others, such as Pwan Yekoo, who appeared in Barnum's Chinese Museum. Rather than promote Sino-American understanding, these women unwittingly initiated the earliest stereotype of Chinese women as exotic curiosities. Therefore, by 1848, when gold was discovered in California, some of the negative images of the Chinese and Chinese women, which would later serve American writers so well, were firmly in place.

With the discovery of gold, men of all nationalities, including the Chinese, flocked to California. Few women accompanied these early immigrants, who expected to earn their fortune and return home. But many of those women who did arrive at the gold fields were prostitutes imported into the area by Chinese and Euro-American men who wished an easy profit. Like slave women who were used to increase their owners' profits, Chinese women too became a lucrative commodity. Many Chinese women were early victims of the system of prostitution, which followed the California gold rush and included women of many nationalities.

The demand for Chinese prostitutes in California was partly the result of the scant supply of Chinese women and the legal prohibition against sexual relations between Euro-American women and Chinese men.[11] Few Chinese women and legal bars to intermarriage made it nearly impossible for Chinese men to marry and raise families. Moreover, Euro-American males believed that Chinese prostitutes intrinsically knew how to please a man. Additionally, there was "the widespread belief, still curiously prevalent among white men, that there are important anatomical differences between the Oriental woman and her Occidental sisters."[12] An estimated 85 percent (of 654) of the Chinese women in San Francisco were prostitutes in 1860, 71 percent (of 2,018) in 1870, and 61 percent (of 2,085) in 1880.[13]

The large percentage of Chinese prostitutes could be attributed to conditions in China and the traditional disregard for females there.[14] These women were victims of an organized trade in which they were kidnapped, lured, or purchased by Chinese "slave" traders. They were brought to the United States, usually through San Francisco, until 1882 when the Exclusion Act was in force.

Upon arrival in San Francisco, the young women, generally between the ages of sixteen and twenty-five, like African slave women, were taken to the barracoon[15] to be turned over to their owners or stripped for inspection and sold to the highest bidder. After being sold, unlike African women, the Chinese women were forced to sign service contracts in which they agreed to prostitute their bodies for a specific term. The contracts stipulated that if a prostitute were ill, two weeks would be added to the length of the contract for each sick day. If the woman tried to run away, she would remain a slave for life.

The menses were considered an illness within the meaning of the agreement, and the slave girl was considered to be incapacitated three or four days each month. Therefore, at least one month was added to every month of servitude under the terms of the contract, in effect, enslaving her in perpetuity. Considering that few could read and write, the terms of the contract were probably not understood. Alone in an alien country with an alien culture and language, they were unable to avoid what awaited them—although a small number succeeded. One of these was Madame Ah Toy (sometimes called Atoy, Achoy, or Ah Choi) who managed to buy her contract and establish her own import business. She later returned to China as a rich woman.[16] But unless a Chinese woman, like a "Black slave [woman] in the nineteenth century, could buy her freedom . . . she remained the property of her procurer."[17]

A number of institutions responded to the plight of the enslaved Chinese women. Many Methodist and Presbyterian missionaries, principally in San Francisco's Chinatown, launched crusades to rescue Chinese prostitutes. In the same way that they interpreted Chinese culture for the American public, Christian missionaries began writing about the Chinese slave girl syndrome.

One of the earliest of these missionary writers was Mrs. Lu Wheat. Wheat's *The Third Daughter* (1906) relates the life of a Chinese girl, Ah Moy, the third daughter of Ching Fo. In a period of drought during the Boxer Rebellion, her father is forced to sell her to the slave trader Quong Lung in order that her brother might survive. The bulk of the novel describes her childhood in the northern province of Honan, China, with emphasis on the misfortune of being female in traditional Chinese society.

Ching Fo's wife had produced only daughters, and this caused him much distress, as daughters were not worthy representatives of the family. After the birth of Ah Moy, he contemplates allowing her to die. But he decides against it, and later his wife gives birth to a son.

At the age of four, Ah Moy must have her feet bound, which is the tradition among the wealthy Chinese. The technique and pain are described at great length, perhaps to illustrate the pain Chinese women suffer in their culture in order to make them more sexually appealing.[18]

When Ah Moy is about twenty years old, a persistent drought in her province is coupled with the Boxer Rebellion. Ah Moy's family-selected fiancé joins the rebellion and is killed. Her family's wealth is rapidly dissipated in the struggle for survival. The father gradually comes to the realization that he must sell Ah Moy in order that the more important family member, the son, might survive. Wheat, with much compassion, intimates that this is a very painful decision for all involved.

Quong Lung, a merchant and slave trader, takes Ah Moy and a Eurasian slave girl, Wing, to Shanghai, but prices have fallen. He then decides to take them to San Francisco where he can demand a higher price. Using forged documents, he expects them to enter the United States without difficulty; however, while on board ship, the two young women are befriended by missionaries who realize that they are slave girls.

Because of certain passport irregularities, they are not immediately allowed to enter the country. The missionaries arrive first and take Ah Moy to their mission home for "fallen women." A highly improbable situation arises: Wing's father has died, and as the only surviving family member, Wing becomes a very wealthy woman. In the meantime, Quong Lung has been busy. He hires a lawyer and takes the missionaries to court. He wins, and Ah Moy is remanded to his custody.

After the court appearance, Ah Moy is taken to the barracoon, where she is stripped and inspected by prospective customers. Overcome with shame and loss of honor, she uses her father's knife, first to kill the prospective buyer, and then herself.

Critics have suggested that Mrs. Lu Wheat is the least patronizing toward Chinese-Americans of any of the missionary writers. She relies on adequate characterization of Ah Moy to convey the sense of tragedy, while at the same time placing the blame for Ah Moy's predicament on society rather than on Ah Moy. Mrs. Wheat is an exception in reproaching society rather than the victim. Later writers seemed to have taken the opposite view.

Charles R. Shepherd was one of the writers who chose not to hold society responsible for the problems of the Chinese in the United States. Although Euro-American critics consider Shepherd's treatment of the Chinese and Chinatown in *The Ways of Ah Sin* (1923) sympathetic, most Chinese-American critics consider it offensive. When *The Ways of Ah Sin* was published, the Native Sons of the Golden State, predecessor of the Chinese-American Citizens Alliance in San Francisco, passed a resolution condemning the book as obscene and inaccurate.

The author, Charles R. Shepherd, was the superintendent of the Chung Mei Home for orphaned Chinese-American boys at El Cerrito, California, for twenty-five years. He uses this position to give added authority to his writing. In the foreword, Shepherd very clearly states his intentions to depict the Chinese in the same manner as Bret Harte, which is as sly and unscrupulous.

Shepherd seems to have misunderstood the meaning and symbolic content of the Bret Harte poem, "Plain Language from Truthful James."[19] Readers like Shepherd wanted to believe the worst interpretation and refused to see the irony, which, according to Harte, was to expose the duplicity of Euro-Americans when dealing with the Chinese. Shepherd apparently accepted the literal meaning of the poem, but while misreading Harte, he does seem to have been aware of the opposition from the Native Sons of the Golden State who apparently had read it correctly. Shepherd creates the impression that any opposition must be from tong members (a fraternal or secret society) or in collusion with them. This foreword to *The Ways of Ah Sin* sets the tone of the book and is not meant to be an apologia.

As previously mentioned, missionaries were responsible for much of the misinformation about the Chinese and Chinatown. Shepherd is a prime example of this presentation of inaccuracies. He sets *The Ways of Ah Sin* in San Francisco in 1920. Ah Mae, the central character, has a very oppressive life in China until she is sold, allegedly to become the concubine of a wealthy Chinese-American. The trader, using illegal documents, enters the United States through San Francisco with Ah Mae, and for fifteen hundred dollars she is placed in the home of Jue Yat, her new owner. While acting as a serving girl at one of his parties she discovers her brother, now a highbinder,[20] who had left China several years before. With Ah Mae's refusal to become Jue Yat's concubine, Jue Yat sells her to another tong member.

Upon recognizing his sister's dangerous position, Ah Mae's brother attempts to rescue her. When his attempts fail, he secretly contacts Catherine McCormack, a fictionalized Donaldina Cameron.[21] Catherine McCormack, like Donaldina Cameron, had undertaken as her life's work the rescue and rehabilitation of "slave" girls. With the help of the police, Mrs. McCormack rescues Ah Mae and takes her to the mission home, where she will learn a trade, the English language, and the American way of life.

Mrs. McCormack liberates another slave girl, Ah Kum. But this rescue is not as easy as Ah Mae's. Ah Kum's owner sues for her return. There is a court appearance that Shepherd uses to reveal much inaccurate and highly inflammatory information about the character of Chinatown.

Shepherd gives negative views of Chinatown similar to those of previous writers. There are crime, opium, vice, tong murders, and kidnapping. The Chinese are portrayed as a subhuman species who gamble incessantly, buy and sell women, and deal in drugs, frequently using children to peddle their opium. Crime and vice are allowed to flourish as long as it is contained within Chinatown. However, this containment required the complicity of authorities, which Shepherd readily acknowledges. There was a saying on the San Francisco police force at this time, "If you are sick financially get on the Chinatown squad and you'll get well quick."[22]

It would have been expected that, given Charles R. Shepherd's training and position, he would have dealt more compassionately with his material. Instead, he chose to highlight the more sensational and lurid aspects of Chinese life in the United States, which may have been accurate but were not representative.

The tongs, about which he wrote so graphically, did and do exist. They were patterned after the secret societies of south China and, on the positive side, offered protection and security to the residents of Chinatown. They also provided medical attention, funeral expenses, job opportunities, and business "protection." Today, tongs are slowly dying out. As more and more Chinese enter the mainstream of American society, there is little need for the services offered by the tong. However, such positive aspects did not make exciting reading. Only the negative criminal aspects, such as prostitution, gambling, and tong wars, caught the imagination of both writers and the reading public.

The illegal activities and exotic character of Chinatown were revealed in the "Yellow Peril"[23] literature of the late nineteenth and early twentieth centuries. It was based on the assumption that Asian immigration would eventually overwhelm the United States. "Yellow Peril" literature captured the imagination of the reading public. Writings by Jack London, Frank Norris, or any of the numerous writers in the *Overland Monthly* of this period fueled such suppositions.

During this period of "Yellow Peril" writing, with few exceptions, female characters were omitted. In his first published short story, "The Haunted Valley" (1871), Ambrose Bierce exposes anti-Chinese attitudes without including a single Chinese character. Jo Dunfer has killed Ah Wee because "he" would not cut down trees correctly. A jury of the townspeople acquits Dunfer. The denouement of the story comes when it is discovered that Ah Wee was actually a woman whom Dunfer had won in San Francisco in a poker game. Originally Dunfer had identified her as a coolie, accidentally killed her, and buried her by his cabin. Ah Wee is one of the earliest representations of Chinese women in American fiction. As property, she is at the mercy of her owner. She is bought, sold, and killed by her "owner," who had no fear of punishment.

Three short stories written by Joseph Hanson and published in the *Overland Monthly* in 1920 and 1921 featured Chinese-American women. "The Winning of Josephine Chang,"[24] one of these, is uncharacteristic of the writing of the period for two reasons. First, it is not influenced by or concerned with the Yellow Peril. Second, both lovers are Chinese-Americans educated and socialized by American society.

Josephine's father, Tin Woo Chang, is a wealthy businessman, and Josephine has a bride-price. Not the usual dowry, the price was the solving of a riddle. The conundrum is hidden in an ancestral jade amulet that Josephine wears. The task of the prospective husband is to solve the riddle. Many try and fail. Yee Kwong, a handsome, university-educated diplomat, is the first suitor whom both father and daughter agree on. The father then arranges for Yee Kwong to solve the riddle. Both Josephine and Yee Kwong, perhaps because of their American education and adoption of American values, do not take the puzzle seriously. However, Josephine does adhere to other traditional Chinese cultural values, for example, allowing herself to be offered for a bride-price. Her father also seems to be acting more for the sake of tradition than for the letter of the law when he rigs the contest in favor of Yee Kwong.

The second story, "Behind the Screen,"[25] serves to reinforce the image of the Chinese woman as prostitute and helpless robot. A beautiful woman is kidnapped in China by the bandit Fook Chang, who renames her The Desert Lily. She is sold to a Tatar priest, who in turn sells her to a traveling Manchu, Ah Fang. Ah Fang takes her from China to Mexico and then to San Francisco. Wing Fo, her betrothed, follows her to the United States, where he goes to Ah Fang to demand her release, but Ah Fang tells him that her price is one thousand dollars. Wing Fo becomes a contract farm laborer in Santa Clara County to earn the sum, but the work proves too arduous for his delicate constitution. In a dream, winning lottery numbers are revealed to him. He plays and wins, but unfortunately the ransom price of the Desert Lily is escalated. Wing Fo decides to kill Ah Fang, but The Desert Lily does it instead by dropping a flower pot on his head. She inherits Ah Fang's substantial fortune and lives happily ever after with Wing Fo.

The Desert Lily works as a prostitute for the procurer, Ah Fang, and this is the very limited role that she plays in the story. She is the cause of the action, but very little is revealed about her. The Desert Lily is merchandise that is bought and sold at the whim of men.

In "The Divorce of Ah Lum,"[26] the third short story by James Hanson, the setting is once again San Francisco's Chinatown. Ah Lum decides to divorce Lin Jen, his wife of many years, because of her lack of beauty, her foul temperament, her refusal to support his gambling habits, and the epithets that she constantly hurls at him: "Skin of a turtle's egg! Slime of an octopus! Breath of a stink-pot!"[27]

Believing himself chased by the tong for obtaining an American divorce, Ah Lum goes into hiding. He is actually being pursued by Lin Jen's new American divorce lawyer, who is demanding alimony. Realizing that alimony is the price one pays when acquiring an American divorce, he decides to return to his wife.

Again, the women are props around whom the story is constructed. They are stick figures rather than rounded characters who are necessary for plot development. Again the focus is on the men, and very little, if anything, is learned about any of these women.

A short story by Margaret Stabler is different. In "The Sale of Sooy Yet: The Story of a Modern Delilah,"[28] the main character, Sooy Yet, is portrayed in greater depth. Man Toy, a wealthy, powerful tong leader, is growing old, and he wants a young wife with whom to spend his declining years. Sooy Yet, who is to be sold in June, has been rejected by a number of suitors because she is plain and bad tempered, though as a woman her value is in her looks. After being on display in the window of her father's restaurant for some time, she decides to take control of the situation. First, she arranges for Man Toy to hear her excellent singing voice without his seeing her. She invites him to dine in her father's restaurant, and while she is serving him, she surreptitiously drops mysterious green crystals into his food. This drug causes a headache, which she massages away. But while she is massaging his forehead, she puts drops into his eyes that cause his blindness. Because of his blindness, Man Toy is forced to leave his position in the tong. At this point, Sooy Yet takes over her own negotiations and manages to obtain a high sale price for herself. Sooy Yet marries Man Toy and keeps him happy with her singing and massages. Periodically she rubs the drops into his eyes to keep him blind so that he will never see her.

Sooy Yet is a rare female portrait in the literature of this period. She is intelligent; she takes control of her own life and does not behave as a helpless robot filled with filial piety. The author tells us that "she was equal to the emergency, for her lack of personal attractiveness was more than balanced by that most unwholesome and unnatural attribute in any woman, yellow or white,—brains."[29]

Of all the negative images of the Chinese prevalent in American literature, perhaps the most enduring is that of the unassimilable alien. Charlie Chan, the Hawaiian police detective created by Earl Derr Biggers, is perhaps the most famous Chinese-American fictional character. Chan considered himself Americanized, yet he suffered under the burden of the dual personality: culturally Chinese and nominally American. As an Americanized Chinese, Chan is a counterfeit American, not a real one. His blending of East and West means he must maintain two separate and apparently inimical identities. During the day he must work within the structure of a Euro-American system without being a part of it, and at night he reverts to a Chinese way of life, complete with gongs, jade, and atonal music. His English, which is not his first language, is flowery, contrived, and almost impossible to follow. Additionally, Chan is outside the Euro-American model of masculinity, frequently being described as dainty or soft. Above all, he remains subservient, effeminate, and unassimilable. Nevertheless, he is a part of American society. Fu Manchu, Sax Rohmer's diabolical criminal, the second most popular yet the most negative Chinese character in American fiction, could never be a part of American society. The only time he made any effort to blend into the American scene was when he plotted to take control of the United States.

This alien image was applied primarily to men but was also used in the depiction of female fictional characters. *Java Head* (1918), a novel by Joseph Hergesheimer that develops the theme of the opposition of East and West, uses this image of the unassimilable female alien.

In *Java Head*, Hergesheimer introduces a new type of Chinese: Taou Yuen, a Manchurian of noble birth. She is not an immigrant; she is not a laborer; she is not a slave girl; she does not settle in the West; and she is not from south China. She marries a sea captain and settles in Salem, Massachusetts.

Gerrit Ammidon, Taou Yuen's sea captain husband, is a completely naive character who surprises his family with his new bride, who not only looks different, dresses exotically, and speaks halting English but is not viewed as human by the other characters. He is surprised when she is not wholly accepted by his family or Salem society. The women of Salem express a more subtle, feminine type of racism. They expected the men to establish sexual relations with Chinese women but not to marry them and bring them home.

But under the circumstances she is treated tolerably well except by Edward Dunsack, the uncle of Gerrit's former love, Nettie Vollar. Dunsack has spent time in China, and from his travels he has acquired the habit of opium smoking. (Curiously, the use of opium is mentioned not in connection with the Chinese but with a Euro-American male.) Dunsack is attracted to Taou Yuen because of the erotic reputation of Chinese women.

Gradually, Gerrit begins to feel that perhaps he should have married his Euro-American lover, Nettie Vollar. Taou Yuen, understanding that he has turned away from her, commits suicide. But rather than accepting responsibility for his role in Taou Yuen's suicide, Gerrit blames a racist United States for her death.

Taou Yuen never assimilated into American culture. She remained Chinese in all aspects of her life and made no attempt to Americanize, which is one of the more blatantly false criticisms of Chinese-Americans. While still in China, she probably did learn only a smattering of English, but rejection by the people of Salem also played an active role in her failure to assimilate. She was culturally foreign, racially different, and religiously non-Christian. Her noble upbringing had no bearing on their decisions to rebuff her. Hergesheimer clearly demonstrates Stuart C. Miller's thesis[30] that anti-Chinese feeling existed throughout the country, not only in the West.

Most writers continued to place their Chinese characters on the Pacific Coast, but not all of them used completely stereotyped characters. Dashiell Hammett (1894–1961), in two books of short stories set in the West, *The Continental Op* and *The Big Knockover*, features Chinese-American characters who operate against the stereotypes. In the novella "Dead Yellow Women" (*The Big Knockover*, 1924), Hammett's opening paragraph provides a description of a character who is entirely different, a fashionable, contemporary Chinese-American woman, Lillian Shan. She is the daughter of a wealthy immigrant from north China who has died, leaving her the sole heir to his fortune and his Pacific Coast mansion. Lillian is at the office of the investigator, the Continental Op, because when she unexpectedly returned from an out-of-town trip, she found her servants dead or missing. She hires the Continental Op to solve the mystery.

In search of information concerning the deaths of Shan's servants, the Op begins his investigation in Chinatown. Here, Hammett resorts to stereotypical depictions: dark, dank, and mysterious. This is the exotic, cryptic Chinatown, with the tunnels and hidden rooms so familiar to readers of "Yellow Peril" fiction.

The Op continues his investigation until he discovers that Lillian Shan and Chang Li Ching, an important Chinatown personage, are working together. Lillian is cooperating with him because Chang is one of the leaders of the anti-Japanese movement in China and is shipping guns illegally through her mansion to patriots there. He makes this discovery in a scene in which Lillian Shan is present, dressed in a spectacularly different manner in ceremonial Chinese attire. Lillian Shan's explanation for her dress and for her presence in Chinatown is that she is where she belongs, in Chinatown with her people.

Hammett presents all the essentials of a fictional Chinatown—tunnels, secret passageways and rooms, slave girls, illegal aliens, drugs—with critical improvements of his own. William Wu maintains that Hammet "presents Lillian Shan as an educated, sophisticated Chinese-American woman, still a rarity in American fiction."[31] Although the staple view of the Chinese villain is present, Hammet has problems with Lillian Shan, who suffers from the writer's concept of a dual personality. Since she cannot be American—Caucasian—she must revert to her Chinese identity. She can only ostensibly, never actually, be an American. Her Chinese ancestry will always thwart her American upbringing and education, which should have provided her with the ability to be culturally American and to be accepted as such, not just as a foreigner in the land of her birth.

The first clearly delineated characterization of a Chinese woman came before the American public not as an American creation but as a British export. She was Fah Lo Suee, the daughter of Fu Manchu. Fu Manchu was the literary invention of Sax Rohmer. Rohmer was born Arthur Henry Ward in Birmingham, England, of Irish parents in 1883. He tried his hand at numerous professions until he settled on writing. Fu Manchu, who became his most successful literary accomplishment, was conceived as the result of an assignment in Limehouse (London's Chinatown);[32] and Fah Lo Suee became the prototype of Asian women for decades to come. She was first introduced in the novel *The Yellow Claw* (1915) as a minor character and reached her full development in *The Daughter of Fu Manchu* (1931).

In the novel, Fah Lo Suee hopes to reorganize her absent father's sinister organization, the Si Fan, which is dedicated to the extermination of the Caucasian race. The character created by Rohmer contains three critical traits: exotic sensuality, sexual weakness for Euro-American men, and a villainous nature.

Fah Lo Suee is gradually introduced to the reader through the other characters as a very attractive, tall, green-eyed Asian woman. Subsequently, her evil nature is revealed. Fah Lo Suee is so unusually dangerous because as the half-caste offspring of Fu Manchu, the result of his affair with a Russian woman, she has adopted her father's Asian methods of assassination, kidnapping, and using mysterious drugs.

When Shan Greville, the bachelor protagonist who is the object of Fah Lo Suee's affections, meets her, she is dressed much the same as Lillian Shan, in ceremonial Chinese attire. Fah Lo Suee herself does not attract Greville; rather, it is the hypnotic quality of her voice that fascinates him. She captures and drugs Greville. On regaining consciousness, he sees her as a marvelously crafted jade statue. Fah Lo Suee tells him of her plans for world domination and of her loneliness, hinting at her love for him. It occurs to him that she "had conceived a sudden characteristically Oriental infatuation."[33] Like many other fictional Asian women, she looks to the Euro-American male for rescue from her oppressive culture. But with her beauty, intelligence, wealth and power, she is not a *real* woman, that is, an Anglo-American woman. Her reactions are not feminine; she smiles when others would have screamed and fainted. Fah Lo Suee is finally defeated by her father and the British agents with whom she has been dueling.

Fah Lo Suee was frequently identified with the Hindu goddess Kâli, the goddess of death and destruction, who is the symbol of the Si Fan. In times past, her ritual demanded human sacrifice. All Asian events, entities, and attributes are evil, and evil is associated with Fah Lo Suee and her father. But Kâli is also the Great Mother and goddess of fertility. Perhaps Rohmer is harking back to the uncontrolled birthrate of Asians, which was one of the primary themes of "Yellow Peril" literature. Along with the perfect beauty of Fah Lo Suee are her high intelligence and consummate evil. Her only weakness is her love for Shan Greville, who eventually assists in her defeat.

Although Fah Lo Suee is the prototype for other Asian women, her name did not become symbolic of all Asian women or of any woman who approaches masculine power. That honor belongs to the Dragon Lady, the creation of cartoonist Milton Caniff. An authoritative, bewitching, obstinate, half-caste Chinese villainess, she first appeared in "Terry and the Pirates" in *The Chicago Tribune* in 1934.

It is not certain how Caniff conceived the name of his villainess. However, the dragon in Western culture differs significantly from the dragon in Chinese culture. For the Chinese, the dragon is a benevolent creature, whereas in Western culture the dragon is Satan's alter ego. In the West, the image of the dragon as a sinister, dangerous, and aggressive monster originated in the Bible. In the twelfth chapter of Revelation, St. Michael the Archangel conquers the dragon (Satan) and his angels and throws them out of heaven. Therefore, from its earliest inception in Western culture, the dragon has been associated with evil.

Nonetheless, the dragon has become a staple literary item with many writers who do not consider it as a monstrous creature, but rather as a beautiful woman with long, flowing hair. In this incarnation, it is even more terrible than in many previous versions because, disguised as a woman, the dragon seems less menacing. Yet, for the Chinese, the dragon's image is antithetical to either Western version.

It is, perhaps, in China where it became the emblem of imperial power that the dragon figure has been most utilized. The Emperors numbered the five-clawed dragon among their ornaments. According to Cirlot, the Chinese dragon symbolizes the "mastering and sublimation of wickedness."[34] For the Chinese, the dragon also represents "the highest level of spirituality; the intermediary plane of the phenomenal life; and the lower level of inferior and telluric forces."[35] A distinctive feature of Chinese culture that the missionaries overlooked was the diametrically opposed symbolism of the Chinese dragon versus the Western one. One only has to see a Chinatown parade to understand the benevolent aspects of the Chinese dragon.

Milton Caniff had to have been aware of this view of the dragon in Chinese culture; his biographer, John Paul Adam, writes that "he read every book on the Orient that he could lay his hands on. . . . [He] interviewed people who knew any thing about the Far East."[36] Thus, Adams considers him an expert on the region. It would seem that even though the character he created is Chinese and the setting is Asia, he would have presented a more balanced view. However, he selected a Western point of view in order to make the Dragon Lady more compelling to his readers.

At the height of its popularity, "Terry and the Pirates" was "syndicated to a hundred and seventy-five newspapers with a combined circulation of seventeen million,"[37] and the comic strip most certainly influenced the United States' reading public in its attitudes toward Asian women. Nevertheless, Caniff, who "had never been nearer the Orient than the corner of Mott and Pell [New York's Chinatown], read some books by Pearl Buck to pick up background materials, invented and named a cast of characters."[38]

The strip concerned the adventures of Terry, a typical American boy whose grandfather had left him a map of an abandoned mine. As a counterbalance to the wholesome Terry, Caniff created an appealing villainess. "Instead of the orthodox oily male, he invented a beautiful half-caste woman who led a gang of river pirates . . . [she was] named the Dragon Lady."[39]

The Dragon Lady, whom Terry first met when he landed in China to search for the mine, is a beautiful, long-legged, ultra-bosomy, almost waistless Eurasian who operates along the China coast. She is as "tough as a hash-heavy top sergeant... [and as] ... tricky as a pair of loaded dice on payday."[40] Similar to her predecessor Fah Lo Suee, her only weakness is her sexual availability to Euro-American men.

In an episode that appeared in 1939 in *The Chicago Tribune*, a group of Chinese farmers have refused to follow the Dragon Lady's orders to execute a group of captured soldiers. She and Pat Ryan, Terry's mentor, have an argument about the farmers' refusal. Ryan reminds her that, after all, she is only a woman, a person who deserves to be ruled by men like Cleopatra or Queen Elizabeth I, who never married, and thus were never conquered. The Dragon Lady becomes very angry and fires her gun at Ryan, but she misses. Ryan then takes the Dragon Lady into his arms and gives her a long, ardent kiss. She drops her pistol and succumbs to the moment. Despite all of her power and intelligence, she proves that she is *just* a woman.

After December 7, 1941, the Dragon Lady fought with Terry against the Japanese in an effort to free China. Through the years, the Dragon Lady's appearance, activities, and enemies changed with the times. In the 1950s, she was active alternately with and against the communists in China; in the 1960s it was uncertain if she were an ally of the French or the Viet Cong in Indo-China. By the 1970s she was operating in the Middle East, involved in oil pipeline schemes. Throughout she remained beautiful, coldly intelligent, and thwarted by Terry and his friends, a fantasy of Asian women created by a Euro-American male writer.

Although Euro-American writers viewed Chinese and Chinese-American women with a stereotypical eye, they did not deal with them much differently than Chinese-American male writers did. There is a certain amount of hostility toward both Chinese women and Chinese-American women in the writings of many Chinese-American male writers. However, Louis Chu, one of the more well-known Chinese-American male writers, reserves his malice for United States–born Chinese women, not the China-born.

Louis Chu was born in 1915 near Canton, China. In 1924 when he was nine years old, his family moved to Newark, New Jersey. He attended school and college in New Jersey, earning a B.A. in English. Later, he received a Master of Arts in sociology from New York University. During World War II he served in the United States Army in southeastern China. Chu visited China again after the war and married there. He was the proprietor of a Chinatown record shop and was the only Chinese disc jockey in New York City until his death in 1971.

Chu's *Eat a Bowl of Tea*, published in 1961, is set in New York's Chinatown at the end of World War II. The title refers to the many cups of bitter herbs Ben Loy must eat in an attempt to cure his impotency.

Ben Loy, the protagonist, leaves his village in China to come to the United States to live with the father whom he has never seen. His father, Wah Gay, is a bitter old man who has lived in the United States for about twenty years, not seeing his wife and family for all this time. When Ben Loy arrives, Wah Gay sends him to Stanton, Connecticut, to work because he realizes that he is unable to guide him along the proper moral path. The old man has spent almost all his time in Chinatown with only a few contacts with Euro-American society, which have been limited to harassment by police and immigration officials and brief encounters with prostitutes.

One snowy night Ben Loy is enticed into accompanying a friend to New York to seek prostitutes. Soon his life assumes the same form as his father's and the other womenless men before him. Before long, Ben Loy begins to visit prostitutes regularly.

Wah Gay sees that Ben Loy has acquired his habits, so he decides that it is time for Ben Loy to marry. The old rice cooker, wife of his friend Lee Gong, has been prodding him to find a husband for their daughter, Mei Oi. Lee Gong proposes that Ben Loy marry her. Ben Loy agrees that a China-born wife is better for him because most women cannot be trusted, especially America-born Chinese women.

Ben Loy goes to China to marry Mei Oi. Instead of leaving her in China, as countless men had done before him, he brings her with him to the United States because times and the laws have changed. Wah Gay is very pleased with his son's decision because he believes that not only are the American-born Chinese women immoral and expensive, they do not make good wives.

After their village marriage and a honeymoon in Hong Kong, the couple returns to New York. There, however, Ben Loy finds himself unable to perform his husbandly duties, ostensibly because of his frequent alliances with prostitutes. He tells the doctor that the cause of his impotency is his many bouts of sexually transmitted diseases. Even so, Mei Oi internalizes his failures and believes herself responsible.

In view of her loneliness caused by few women friends, a strange language, and an alien culture and her self-doubt, Mei Oi is induced into an affair with Jo Ah Song, a predatory old bachelor. Not only does she become an adulteress, she becomes pregnant.

The adultery and pregnancy soon become public knowledge among the Chinatown residents. Curiously, it is the men who continually gossip about Mei Oi's predicament. Ben Loy is paralyzed by the events. The adultery does not distress him as much as Mei Oi's lack of discretion; therefore, his father decides to take action. In an attempted assassination, he severs Ah Song's ear. Ah Song presses charges, forcing Wah Gay to go into hiding in New Jersey.

The tong puts pressure on Ah Song to withdraw the charges against Wah Gay or face five years' banishment from Chinatown. Since Ah Song is alone in the United States with no members of his clan to defend him, he capitulates. Ben Loy and Mei Oi move to San Francisco to avoid the loss of face in New York. Ben Loy eats several bowls of bitter tea, which he gets from a San Francisco herbalist, and regains his sexual ability. He cheerfully accepts the new baby as his own.

Chu's Chinatown is an area in New York caught between China and the United States, between the old ways and the new. In an attempt to apply Chinese traditional values in the United States, the community of aging bachelors fails miserably. These values were the only ones they had, as they had not formulated new ones to help make sense of their new condition. Their Chinatown is not the Chinatown of curio shops and exotic foods but of grimy basement rooms, arduous toil, mah-jongg parlors, and gossip. This Chinatown is a drab, dingy ghetto where old men gamble and watch their dreams slowly fade. There are no tunnels, secret passageways, or slave girls, only lonely men who try to impose their remembered values on an eighteen-year-old girl.

Mei Oi becomes a victim of this sterile, limited world where men entertain lustful thoughts about their friends' wives and daughters. Even Chin Yuen, Ben Loy's friend, amuses himself with thoughts about Mei Oi and the family life he has missed. Despite his reputation, Ah Song was one of their faithful companions. Ben Loy's impotency is more than his personal tragedy; it is symbolic of Chinatown, a limited area filled with lonely, aging bachelors who were forced by racist laws to leave their wives in China. Not only are they impotent but also destitute of any hope.

Mei Oi has been plucked from her village in China, where she at least enjoyed cultural comfort, and set down in New York. Not only does she have to meet the expectations of the men of the community who have higher standards for her than of America-born Chinese women, but she must also produce male children with an impotent husband. If she does not produce offspring, she will again be stigmatized, this time for being barren. Her participation in the affair with Jo Song cannot be justified because it violates the sanctity of her marriage, but her unfaithfulness is ironic because she was chosen to be the ideal wife since she was *not* American. Even her name, Mei Oi, "beautiful love," suggests that she should have been the perfect wife.

Chinese-American wives in the short stories of Jeffery Paul Chan receive even harsher treatment than Mei Oi. Chan was born in Stockton, California, in 1942. His short stories have appeared in *West* magazine, *Asian-American Authors, Seeing Through the Shuck,* and *Bulletin of Concerned Asian Scholars.*

Exploring anti-Sinicism in Nevada in "Jackrabbitt," Chan depicts a contemporary world in which Chinese women are still bought, sold, or traded for sexual purposes without impunity. Frankie, a young Chinese-American man, explains to Pete, his boss, that his mother abandoned the family to become a prostitute in San Francisco's Chinatown. The negative image of Chinese-American women continues in Chan's "The Chinese in Haifa." In the narrative, Bill Wong's newly divorced wife, Alice, becomes a coolie driver, a greedy, grasping woman who takes everything. After taking a shower, he has to dry himself with bathroom tissue because she has taken all the towels. Alice, his ex-wife, is a Chinese-American female Fagin who steals his children, teaches them Chinese, and teaches them to hate him. When he says, "God in heaven, I'm free," it is not clear whether he is free from his ex-wife or from her constant reminder of his "Chinese-ness." Bill Wong is a college teacher who lives in the suburbs, smokes marijuana, and likes blintzes. Alice is described as a Chinese vampire with soy sauce instead of blood dribbling down her jaws. While fishing, he fantasizes that Alice is the hooked fish, and as he lands the fish he thinks to himself, "Die, Alice." The fish that he landed was a capizone, known for its grotesque appearance.

While he is extremely critical of everything about his ex-wife, he is equally as admiring of his Jewish neighbor's green-eyed, blonde wife with whom he is having an affair. She represents all the beauty and good that is not found in Chinese-American culture and in Chinatown. His attitude toward Chinese-American women corresponds to his attitude toward Chinatown. For Chan, Chinatown is a zoo, or, as in the "Chinese in Haifa," a chicken coop.

The chicken coop metaphor for Chinatown is continued by Frank Chin. Frank Chew Chin, the most prolific Chinese-American male writer (short story writer, essayist, and playwright), is a distinctive example of a writer possessing vehement sentiments toward Chinese-American women and Chinatown. Born in 1940 in Berkeley, California, he claims to have been the first Chinese-American brakeman on the Southern Pacific Railroad.

In his writings two main themes appear: the feminization of Chinese-American men and the Christianization of Chinese-American history. These themes are usually centered around the coming of age of a young Chinese-American male and his alienation from Chinatown. Unlike C. Y. Lee's exotic Chinatown in *The Flower Drum Song*, Chin's Chinatown is metaphorically a chicken coop: a dirty, noisy, foul-smelling place occupied by people who speak an undecipherable language and who, for him, are depicted as insects, spiders, and frogs.

In "Food for All His Dead," Johnny shares a terrible secret with his father: the old man is dying of tuberculosis, and no one must know. The old man is symbolically Chinatown, which is also dying, although the residents refuse to acknowledge it. Chinatowns are the products of Euro-American racism. Chin has written "that the Chinese themselves clustered together to preserve their alien culture is for him a myth: The railroads created a detention camp and called it 'Chinatown.' "[41]

The inhabitants of Chinatown are less than human. In "Give the Enemy Sweet Sissies and Women to Infatuate Him, and Jades and Silks to Blind Him with Greed," the images of the residents of Chinatown are swarms of bluebottle flies and crickets. The same insect imagery is continued in "Food for All His Dead." Animal imagery is applied to Chinese mothers, who become chimpanzee-cute women who speak English like Daffy Duck.

Even Johnny's girlfriend, Sharon, has a frog-like stare with eyelashes that quiver like an insect's antennae and skin that is more animal-like than human. Johnny has outgrown not only Chinatown but also Chinese women. Johnny's girlfriend does not understand the meaning of his words. Like the stereotype of the Chinese, Sharon's English skills are deficient, but she understands her place as a woman very well. Chin's depiction of Chinese-American women is similar to African-American male writers' depictions of African-American women. His portrayals of women do not deviate significantly from the stereotypes created by the dominant culture. Chinese-American women are compared to Euro-American women and are found to be lacking in beauty and culture.

Johnny and the other male characters evolve into one character, Tam Lum, in Chin's first play, *The Chickencoop Chinaman*, produced in New York at the American Place Theater in 1972. The play depicts the cultural and historical dilemma of Tam Lum, a young Chinese-American writer and documentary film maker. Tam is insecure in his cultural identity and his place in the wider American history and society.

The play opens with Tam on a plane en route to Pittsburgh to interview Charley Popcorn as part of a documentary film that he is making on the life of ex-boxer Ovaltine Jack Dancer. The flight attendant, the Hong Kong Dream Girl, is an Asian, with the hair of Jackie Kennedy and the body of a Dallas Cowboy cheerleader. Tam cannot relate to the flight attendant or any other woman directly, only through sexual innuendo.

Identical to the Hong Kong Dream Girl is a glamourous, sexy, mindless tramp, Lee. As the main female character, Lee is a castrator similar to the African-American Sapphire. She is biracial, possibly passing. She has given birth to several children of several different racial mixtures but mothers only one, her son, Robbie.

As with the Hong Kong Dream Girl, Tam can only relate to Lee sexually. When she reproaches him for refusing to shake Robbie's hand, Tam's only counter is "Wanna fuck?"[42] Later, when Lee discovers that Tam's ex-wife is Caucasian, she denounces him as being effeminate. Supposedly Euro-American women accept Chinese-American men for their love and knowledge of silk, jade and porcelain, not for themselves. To Chin these cultural pursuits are not masculine. Additionally, Chin believes this lack of masculinity is imposed on Chinese-American men by Euro-American society. The rate of marriages outside of the group is frequently used by Chin to support the claim that Chinese-American women accept their alleged effeminancy, which supposedly can be seen in the growing rate of out-marriage by Chinese-American women.

The emasculation and feminization of Chinese-American males, a favorite theme of Frank Chin, is stressed in *The Chickencoop Chinaman*. In this play, he seems to dramatize what he has written in his essays: that the stereotype of Chinese-American men positions them outside the John Wayne mold of Euro-American masculinity.

Tam is vitriolic about his Chinese-American identity, insisting that Chinese-Americans are creations of Euro-American racists. He believes that this same racist mentality has assigned Helen Keller as the metaphor for Chinese-Americans because she sees no evil, hears no evil, speaks no evil. Helen Keller overcame her handicaps not by rioting, protesting, or sitting in but by passively accepting her handicaps to become a model American citizen. Asian-Americans in emulation of her should overcome their racial handicaps to become the "model minority."

A western hero, the Lone Ranger, is the idol of Tam's youth because the mask hid the Ranger's Asian eyes. The Lone Ranger as a Westerner with a long history of anti-Chinese sentiment arrogantly assigns Tam and all other Chinese-Americans to their place in American history as "honorary whites."

In spite of the Lone Ranger's designation of Chinese as "honorary whites," old stereotypes still lingered. One of the persistent stereotypes of

Chinese-American women has been that of the submissive prostitute. Chin acknowledges this image when he has Tam and "Blackjack" Kenji go to a pornographic movie house in search of Charley Popcorn. They look inside the auditorium and see the screen, whereupon Kenji asks Tam, "She [the woman in the pornographic movie] Chinese or Japanese?"

The women in *The Chickencoop Chinaman* play auxiliary roles. They are cheap, stupid tramps or malicious, cruel, promiscuous, castrating women. There does not seem to be any middle ground for Chinese-American women. However, in this play, Chin does not accuse them of killing off the group by out-marriages. He saves that for his second play, *The Year of the Dragon*.

In *The Year of the Dragon* (1974), Chin presents three distinctive types of the Chinese woman: China Mama, the old, traditional, China-born wife who was left behind when Pa Eng came to the United States; Ma, Pa Eng's second United States–born Chinese wife; and Pa's thoroughly acculturated daughter, Mattie.

China Mama is Eng's first wife. Because of his imminent death, Pa Eng has brought her to the United States so that he can die in the arms of his complete Chinese family. She is a model of selfless devotion whose entire life has been dedicated to doing exactly as Pa wished. She is the mother of Fred, the older son, and a paragon of motherhood, although she has been separated from Fred since childhood. She has waited patiently for Pa Eng while he was in the United States, married to another woman. When Fred complains of sore feet from running his Chinatown tourist agency, China Mama immediately brings a tub of warm water in which to soak his feet. She knows her "place" as a proper Chinese woman.

But Fred has little respect for any of the women in the family. He constantly uses expletives with Ma, the second wife, who does not handle stress well. When confronted with a threatening situation, Ma either hides in the bathroom or begins to sing. Ma is very proud of Sis because she is one of a very few Chinese-American babies born in San Francisco in 1938, which is an allusion to the previous lack of women in Chinatown. But now she receives little respect from Pa Eng; he has brought China Mama, his first wife, into the house.

In reaction to this situation or any other situation that she chooses not to confront, not only does Ma retreat to the bathroom or sing; her language becomes confused. Her language abounds with malapropisms. Although Chinese-American, she is unsure of what being Chinese entails. "She's Susie Wong and Flower Drum Song."[43] Ma is also aware of Chinese-American history and the precarious position she is placed in when she marries Pa. American law demanded loss of citizenship and possible deportation for any woman who married a Chinese man.

Sis is a third kind of Chinese woman. She has escaped Chinatown, published a successful cookbook, and married a Euro-American man, of whom Pa does not approve. Her brother, Fred, turns the rate of Chinese "out-marriage" into a joke when he tells Mattie's intended it is the rule, not the exception, for Chinese-Americans to marry outside of their group.

But neither Pa's nor Fred's disapproval is important to Sis; she feels uncomfortable in Chinatown. She does not want Chinatown or being Chinese-American to influence her life. In her naiveté, she wants to forget her history and culture and to be accepted as a person.

Chin continues with his zoo metaphor, representing Chinatown as a private preserve for an endangered species, with Ross, Sis's husband, as the park ranger. This version of Chin's Chinatown is peopled with animals who are not fully aware that they are in the United States instead of China and that therefore they are not Chinese but Chinese-American. They are an invisible people who have been made into a model minority as a counter against other racial or ethnic groups.

In his short stories and plays, Chin created women who are stupid, emasculating, or ashamed of their ethnicity. His women have so internalized the stereotypical view of Chinese-American men as being effeminate that they are out-marrying at alarming rates. They, like their creator, are insecure and uncomfortable with the Chinese element of their cultural identity.

Many Chinese-American male writers paralleled Chin, who like their Euro-American counterparts tended to concentrate on the accomplishments of men, thus relegating women to a subordinate role. On those occasions when women are recognized, the trend seems to continue the Euro-American stereotype of Chinese-American women. Euro-American male writers devalued Chinese women, so Chinese-American men in their rush to become part of the patriarchy, similar to African-American men, also devalued Chinese-American women.

Chin's ultimate insult to women is the protagonist's name in *The Chickencoop Chinaman*, Tam Lum. Tam is a sobriquet for Tampax. "I speak the natural born ragmouth speaking a motherless bloody tongue" (7). For Chin the most important characteristic of Chinese-American women is their total acceptance of the Chinese-American male as effete, an acceptance shown by their rate of out-marriage.

These writers have contributed to a view of Chinese-American women as sexually permissive and at the same time espouse a theory of female inferiority. This inferiority is deeply rooted in a racist system that routinely categorizes women of color according to their alleged sexuality. The images and history of Chinese and Chinese-American women strongly identify them with African-American women. Images created for African-American women seemingly have been applied to many women of color. However, images, positive or negative, are not immutable; they may be altered or adapted according to a society's needs. The images of Chinese-American women seemingly have changed. Nevertheless, the contemporary image of the hard-working, well-educated Asian woman does not always have a basis in fact.

The original images are resilient. Advertisements that range from Asia-based airlines to urban bath houses to the resurgence of mail-order Asian brides testify to the endurability of the original characterizations. The image of the Chinese-American woman has evolved from the submissive, obedient "slave" girl to the competent, hard-working, well-educated contemporary woman and back to the original image.

NOTES

1. Henry Shih-shan Tsai, *The Chinese Experience in America* (Bloomington: Indiana University Press, 1986), 1.

2. An insurgency in China (1850–1864) led by Hung-siu-tsuen who sought to replace the Manchu Dynasty with a native dynasty called the T'ai-ping Chao (Great Peace Dynasty). It was suppressed with the aid of a corps of Chinese led by Charles Gordon George.

3. Stuart C. Miller, *The Unwelcome Immigrant. The American Image of the Chinese, 1785–1882* (Berkeley: University of California Press, 1969), 76.

4. Ibid., 80.

5. Another equally relevant definition of the sojourner is "a stranger in a foreign land who clings to the culture of his own ethnic group, and, although he spends much time in a foreign land, remains unassimilated." Franklin Ng, "The Sojourner, Return Migration and Immigration History," *Chinese America: History and Perspectives, 1987*:58.

6. Ibid.

7. Shehui Ku, "The Bitter Society," trans. June Mei et al., *Amerasia Journal* 8 (1981): 33–68.

8. An anti-Chinese activist whose slogan was, "The Chinese must go!"

9. Marina Heung, "Film Assails Asian Stereotypes," *National Association of Women's Studies* 2 (1989): 9.

10. Judy Yung, *Chinese Women in America: A Pictorial History* (Seattle: University of Washington Press, 1986), 14.

11. Pauli Murray, ed., *State Laws on Race and Color* (Cincinnati: Women's Division of Christian Service Board of Missions and Church Extension, Methodist Church, 1950), lists the following state laws that apply to Asians:

Arizona—Section 63.107 of the Civil Code. "The marriage of persons of Caucasian blood, or their descendants, with Negroes, Hindus, Mongolians, members of the Malay race, or Indians and their descendants shall be null and void."

California—Section 60 of the Civil Code enacted in 1872 and amended in 1905. "The marriages of white persons with Negroes, Mongolians, members of the Malay race, or mulattoes are illegal and void."

Idaho—Section 32.206 of the Civil Code enacted in 1867. "All marriages hereafter contracted of white persons with mongolians [sic], negroes [sic], and mulattoes are illegal."

Missouri—Section 3361 of the Civil Code. "All marriages between white persons and negroes [sic] . . . and Mongolians . . . are prohibited and declared absolutely void."

Montana—Section 5701 of the Civil Code is very specific. "Marriage between a white and Chinese person is void."

Oregon—Section 63.02 of the Civil Code enacted in 1866 states that "it shall not be lawful within this state for any white person . . . to intermarry with a negro [sic], Chinese, or any person having one-fourth or more negro [sic] Chinese, Kanaka [a native Hawaiian or a South Sea Islander] blood. . . . All such marriages shall be absolutely null and void."

North Dakota—Section 14.0106. "The following marriages are null and void from the beginning: The intermarriage or illicit cohabitation of any person belonging to the African, Korean, Malayan or Mongolian race with any person of the opposite sex belonging to the Caucasian or white race."

Utah—Sections 40, 41, 42. "The following marriages are prohibited and declared void. . . . Between a negro [sic] and a white person. . . . Between a Mongolian, member of the malay [sic] race or a mulatto, quadroon, or octoroon, and a white person."

Virginia—Section 20.54. "Unlawful for any white person in this State to marry any save a white person, or a person with no other admixture of blood than white and American Indian."

Wyoming—Section 50.108. "All marriages of white persons with Negroes, Mulattoes, Mongolians or Malaya [sic] hereafter contracted in the State of Wyoming are and shall be illegal and void."

12. Herbert Asbury, *The Barbary Coast. An Informal History of the San Francisco Underworld* (New York: Capricorn Books, 1968), 174.

13. Lucy Cheng Hirata, "Free, Indentured, Enslaved: Chinese Prostitutes in Nineteenth-Century America," *Signs* (Fall 1979): 43.

14. Pearl S. Buck argues in "America's Medieval Women," *Harpers Magazine* (August 1938): 225–32, that women are less respected in the United States than in China.

15. A barrack or enclosure for the confinement of slaves, also known as the auction block or Queen's Room. The barracoon was a closely guarded room large enough to house fifty to one hundred women. In the barracoon, women, like livestock, were put on display for sale.

16. Asbury, 179.

17. Ruth Rosen, *The Lost Sisterhood. Prostitution in America, 1900–1918* (Baltimore: Johns Hopkins University Press, 1982), 122.

18. Sterling Seagrave, *The Soong Dynasty* (New York: Perennial Library, 1985), 158–60.

19. Bret Harte, *The Complete Poetical Works* (New York: P. F. Collier and Sons, 1898), 129–31.

Shepherd was not alone in misinterpreting Harte. Harte has been accused by many of propagating much of the anti-Sinicism that was prevalent. The accusation was based on the actions of Ah Sin in the poem. In the beginning of the poem, Truthful James and Bill Nye get Ah Sin into a "small game of euchre," which they are sure he does not understand.

> Yet the cards they were stacked
>   In a way that I grieve,
> And my feelings were shocked
>   At the state of Nye's sleeve:
> Which was stuffed full of aces and bowers
>   And the same with intent to deceive.

Ah Sin, however, beats the Americans at their own game, and in the same way. He, too, has hidden his cards:

> Then I looked up at Nye.
>   And he gazed upon me;
> And he rose with a sigh,
>   And said, "Can this be?
> We are ruined by Chinese cheap labour;"
>   And he went for that heathen Chinee . . .
> Which is why I remark,
>   And my language is plain,
> That for ways that are dark
>   And for tricks that are vain,
> The heathen Chinee is peculiar,—
>   Which the same I am free to maintain.

The success of these verses was immediate and great; the poem was peddled throughout San Francisco; it went through four editions in England the first year. Posters containing the lines "we are ruined by Chinese cheap labour" were circulated, and Californians jubilantly took up the refrain. Although no impassioned champion of the Chinese, Harte always maintained that his poem was misinterpreted.

20. *Highbinder* is slang dating from 1860, which is thought to be from "hell bender." It describes a member of a secret society of blackmailers said to exist among the Chinese in California and other parts circa 1887.

21. Shepherd dedicated his novel to missionary Donaldina Cameron, celebrated in Christian Chinatown history as "Chinatown's Avenging Angel."

22. Charles R. Shepherd, *The Ways of Ah Sin. A Composite of Things As They Are* (New York: Fleming H. Revell Company, 1923), 109.

23. Oddly, a German autocrat, Kaiser Wilhelm II, is credited with coining the catch phrase that articulated the fear of an inundation of Western nations by

Asians. He used the expression "Yellow Peril" (*gelbe gefahr*) to stir the fear of Russians about the possibility of a new Mongol invasion from the East.

24. Joseph Hanson. "The Winning of Josephine Chang," *Overland Monthly* 75 (June 1920): 493.

25. Joseph Hanson, "Behind the Devil Screen," *Overland Monthly* 77(November 1921): 19–24, 65–66.

26. Joseph Hanson, "The Divorce of Ah Lum," *Overland Monthly* 35 (March 1921): 35.

27. Ibid.

28. Marguerite Stabler, "The Sale of Sooy Yet," *Overland Monthly* 35 (May 1900): 414.

29. Ibid., 415.

30. Stuart C. Miller, *The Unwelcome Immigrant. The American Image of the Chinese, 1785–1882* (Berkeley: University of California Press, 1969). Miller argues that anti-Chinese attitudes were not confined to the West Coast but were national in scope.

31. William Wu, *The Yellow Peril* (Hamden, CT: Archon Books, 1986), 190.

32. Similar views of Chinatown and the Chinese can be found in the writings of Thomas Burke who sets his short stories in Limehouse, London's Chinatown: *Limehouse Nights* (New York: Robert McBride, 1917), *More Limehouse Nights* (New York: George H. Doran, 1921), *Nights in London* (New York: Holt, 1916), *A Tea-Shop in Limehouse* (Boston: Little, 1931), and *Twinkletoes: A Tale of Limehouse* (New York: Robert McBride, 1918). Famed British mystery writer Agatha Christie also set one of her Hercule Poirot novels in Limehouse, *The Big Four* (1927). The Chinese were not the only group disparaged by Christie. *And Then There Were None* (1939) was published outside the United States as *Ten Little Niggers*.

Jay Gelzer's *The Street of a Thousand Delights* (New York: Robert M. McBride and Company, 1922), which is set in Melbourne, Australia's Chinatown, is particularly interesting. She concentrates on the Eurasian and the conflicts that biraciality causes. According to Mrs. Gelzer, the two bloods wage war within the bodies of the Eurasian, causing irreparable psychic damage.

33. Sax Rohmer, *Daughter of Fu Manchu* (New York: Pyramid, 1961 [1931]), 105.

34. J. E. Cirlot, *A Dictionary of Symbols* (New York: Philosophical Library, 1962), 83.

35. Ibid., 84.

36. John Paul Adams, *Milton Caniff. Rembrandt of the Comic Strips* (Philadelphia: David McKay Company, 1946), 41.

37. John Bainbridge, "Significant Sig and the Funnies," *New Yorker* (January 8, 1944): 25.

38. Ibid., 26.

39. Ibid.

40. Ibid.

41. Frank Chin, *The Chickencoop Chinaman and the Year of the Dragon* (Seattle: University of Washington Press, 1981), 5.
    42. Ibid., 12.
    43. Ibid., 126.

Chapter Five

Sui Sin Far to Amy Tan

None of the previously mentioned Chinese-American male writers created more than one-dimensional female characters. For the most part, they have been concerned with "defining themselves as men and with exploring the relationships between their identities as men and their status as members of the Asian American minority."[1] This position cannot be attributable to a male supremacist attitude but rather to the fact that the "Asian American experience has been largely male, shaped by racially discriminatory policies that have undermined their sexual and social status."[2]

Nonetheless, Asian-American men have implicitly demanded, as have African-American men, that a woman's first loyalty should be to eradicating the racism that affects the group rather than to the sexism that affects her. Chinese-American women writers have struggled since the end of the nineteenth century to portray themselves accurately—not as the docile and seductive stereotypes found in male fiction but as fully developed characters with human rather than racial reactions. Sui Sin Far was one of the first.

Edith Eaton, author, known in the East as Sui Sin Far, the "Chinese Lily," died. ... She was the daughter of Edward Eaton ... [who] ... went to the Orient ... [where] ... he became fascinated with the East, and after a year married a Japanese noblewoman.[3]

So reads the obituary that fictionalizes the life of Edith Eaton as created by her sister Winnifred. Under Winnifred's rearrangement of facts, Edith is no longer a Chinese Eurasian but a Japanese Eurasian.

Sui Sin Far (1867–1914) was the daughter of a Chinese mother (Grace Trefusius, Lotus Blossom, 1847–1922) and a British father (Edward Eaton, 1839–1915). The family moved constantly until they reached Montreal, Canada, where Sui Sin Far was born. Eventually, they settled in Hudson City, New York.

Sui Sin Far was a sickly child whose illnesses were exacerbated by the cruelty and racism to which she was exposed. The exposure to bigotry motivated her to write in her memoirs, "Leaves from the Mental Portfolio of an Eurasian,"

I have come from a race on my mother's side which is said to be the most stolid and insensible to feeling of all races, yet I look back over the years and see myself so keenly alive to every shade of sorrow and suffering that it is almost a pain to live. . . . Why is my mother's race despised? I look into the faces of my father and mother. Is she not every bit as dear and good as he? Why? Why?[4]

She cringed at her first sight of Chinese people, but she gradually developed an appreciation and love for her mother's people and began to use them in her writing. In her magazine articles and short stories, she chose to concentrate on the Chinese in the United States rather than embrace a distant, exotic China. This choice was made despite the fact that she had been advised to emphasize her ethnicity through her dress and the use of Confucian quotations in her speech

Sui Sin Far became "one of the first to speak for an Asian-American sensibility that was neither Asian nor white American."[5] By choosing a Chinese pseudonym (Sui Sin Far or "Chinese Lily"), she clearly demonstrated her pride in her heritage. As a Chinese-American writer, she had to find a technique that would enable her to deal with her own experiences, but to do so was to fall outside the mainstream of American writing.

Fictional and grossly distorted stereotypes of the Chinese and Chinatown had already been well established. It became her task to write against these fixed images. Her intention became "not to exploit but rather to record, explain and somehow give meaning to the experience of the Chinese in America."[6]

Her body of writing was very small: one book, *Mrs. Spring Fragrance* (a collection of short stories), and other short stories published individually in national magazines. A *New York Times* review of *Mrs. Spring Fragrance* stated that

[she] has struck a new note in American fiction. She has not struck it very surely. But it has taken courage to strike it at all. . . . The thing she has tried to do is to

portray for readers of the white race the lives, feelings, sentiments of the Americanized Chinese of the Pacific Coast.[7]

She was at her best when writing about women. Her women characters differed from the characters created by non-Chinese writers, who tended to be monolithic, conforming to the stereotypical images of evil, passivity, and sexuality. Sui Sin Far's women characters exhibit a type of individuality that is not found in other characters. According to Chinese tradition, a woman "has to obey (1) her father when young, (2) her husband when married and (3) her son when widowed. She is submissive to her husband or society."[8] Sui Sin Far's women obey or disobey these dicta at will.

In "The God of Restoration," Sie is the daughter of a slave in China who has been betrothed to Koan-lo the first, a wealthy San Francisco businessman. She has come to the United States to marry the older man because her marriage will emancipate her father. On her arrival in San Francisco, she is met at the dock by Koan-lo the second. They had been lovers in China because "in China the daughters of slaves are allowed far more liberty than girls belonging to a higher class of society."[9]

Sie mistakes Koan-lo the second for Koan-lo the first and they marry. When she discovers her error, she goes to Koan-lo the first and pleads that she be allowed to serve him as his slave until the marriage debt is repaid. In this way her father will still receive his freedom. Sie is a virtuous daughter whose primary duty is to her father and not to herself. For her father, she willingly sacrifices herself to Koan-lo the first and abandons her new husband along with her new life.

Similar to Sie are the two self-sacrificing female characters, Mermei and Sin Far, in "The Chinese Lily." Mermei is crippled and badly scarred because of a childhood accident. She and her brother, Lin John, live in the same building as Sin Far (Chinese Lily). One night there is a fire in the building, but the ladder can allow only one to be saved. Mermei tells Sin Far to escape because Lin John loves her, but Sin Far refuses. Sin Far dies; Mermei survives. Sin Far's sacrifice of her life for that of her friend exemplifies two conventional concepts: loyalty to friends and loyalty to lovers. Not only does Sin Far's act complete her duty to Lin John, "her act enables him to fulfill his brotherly duty to take care of his crippled sister. Sin Far is, in every sense, a traditional selfless woman who lives and dies not for herself but for others."[10]

The rebellious women are more numerous and more interesting than the traditional women. Two examples will be used here.

On the surface, Fin Fan, in "The Prize China Baby," seems a traditional woman. She works in her husband's tobacco shop. The only joy in her dreary life is her baby, Jessamine Flower. Chung kee, her husband, resents Jessamine Flower since she demands so much of Fin Fan's time. By working twice as hard, Fin Fan is able to earn as much money as she had previously. She had been a domestic slave who was sold to Chung kee, and nothing in her life had changed: "Though a wife, she was still a slave"(215).

Chung kee uses the threat of giving Jessamine Flower to another woman to maintain his control over Fin Fan, and she usually obeys. However, one day, Fin Fan learns that there is to be a beautiful baby contest at the mission. She decides to enter Jessamine Flower. Chung kee discovers her absence and tells one of the old women who works in the factory to carry the baby to the herb doctor's wife that night. However, while returning from the contest where the baby has won first prize, Fin Fan is struck and killed by a butcher's cart.

Fin Fan's decision to disregard her husband's threats becomes the incentive that gives her strength. She defiantly becomes her own person, but in finding inner strength to disobey her husband, she causes the death of herself and her child. In death she has peace, freedom, and escape from her oppressive husband and the bonus of never being separated from her child.

Pau Lin's problems in "The Wisdom of the New" are different from those of Fin Fan. Pau Lin must deal with both her jealousy of Adah Charlton, the Euro-American woman whom she believes is her rival, and her need to adjust to her new environment. Pau Lin is the illiterate China-born wife of Wou Sankwei. He has not seen her or his son for the seven years that he has been in San Francisco.

When Sankwei goes to meet Pau Lin at the dock, he is accompanied by Adah Charlton and her aunt, Mrs. Dean. Immediately Pau Lin's suspicions are aroused because platonic relationships between men and women were not a part of Chinese tradition.

Resistant to anything new or different, Pau Lin refuses to become Americanized. Although she dotes on her young son, she punishes him because he speaks English after she has cautioned him not to. Later, a second son is born to Pau Lin and Sankwei, but the child dies after his portrait is painted by Adah Charlton. In her ignorance, Pau Lin believes Adah's painting is the cause of the child's death.

Sankwei is constantly in the company of his American friends. Whenever he needs advice or wishes to make decisions that concern his family, he goes to them. Sankwei never considers Pau Lin as intelligent as Adah, and so he never consults his wife.

The incident that most provokes Pau Lin is the cutting of Little Lin's queue. Because Pau Lin thinks Sankwei has done this for Adah, her jealousy becomes more intense. Coupled with Sankwei's seeming eradication of her son's Chinese identity, it causes her to react violently. To prevent what she feels is the Americanization of her son, she poisons the child. Her act forces Sankwei to return with her to China.

Pau Lin is similar to Mei Oi in Louis Chu's *Eat a Bowl of Tea*. She is besieged by the strange cultural environment in which she has been placed. Her husband is insensitive to her feelings and her needs. He never encourages her to become more Americanized; instead he leaves her alone, making all the family decisions without her participation and placing his American friends and their opinions above hers. She is expected to be the proper, traditional Chinese wife in an unfamiliar cultural milieu. Her child, who accompanied her from China, is her only comfort and companion in this strange environment. Seeing her son's Americanization, she feels that she is losing him as she "lost" Sankwei. She reacts from her cultural perspective in order to save him. Although Sankwei's immediate understanding seems highly improbable, nevertheless Pau Lin succeeds; she and Sankwei return to China permanently. Neither she nor Sankwei seems to realize that traditional Chinese customs might not adapt well in an American environment.

While Pau Lin's problems are with the Americanization process, Mrs. Spring Fragrance from the short story of the same name is a thoroughly Americanized Chinese. She arrives in Seattle from China not speaking a word of English, but after five years her English is almost perfect. Mrs. Spring Fragrance is flattered when she is told that she is just like an American woman. She wears Western clothes and is always happy and carefree, although maintaining her cheerfulness must have been difficult, for she had miscarried twice. Mrs. Spring Fragrance has such an overpowering personality that her husband, whose given name is Sing Yook, is referred to as *Mr.* Spring Fragrance.

Most of her neighbors are Euro-American women, and to them she is a source of amusement, a pet. The adjective *little* is used frequently in reference to her; she is a nonthreatening, exotic curiosity.

Sui Sin Far, like many African-American women writers of the period, could not appear too militant in support of her people. She had to modify her stances on racism and sexism to make her writings more palatable to her Euro-American reading audience. Therefore, Mrs. Spring Fragrance handles racism and sexism very delicately. A Euro-American friend has taken her to a lecture in San Francisco, "America the Protector of China." Describing the speech in a letter to her husband who has remained at home,

Mrs. Spring Fragrance skillfully uses in her account the hypocrisy of racism in California. She briefly alludes to the immigration policy of the United States concerning the Chinese and quietly reminds her husband of his male superiority. Although Americanized, Mrs. Spring Fragrance must maintain the facade of a traditional Chinese wife.

In her collection of short stories, *Mrs. Spring Fragrance*, and in her other writings, Sui Sin Far created many female characters—Euro-American, Chinese-American, and Eurasian. Her Chinese-American characters cover a broad spectrum, since it was her ambition to dispel myths and stereotypes and to replace them with more accurate portrayals of her mother's people.

In many of her stories, Sui Sin Far illustrates the exploitation and victimization of women by domineering and authoritarian men. Although she ascribes these traits solely to Chinese men, they seem to be universal ones. The women's dependence on these men is the source of their pain. Yet because of the time and the environment, many of these women never question their subjugation. Sui Sin Far herself went against the dictates of the times for women: she remained single when the married state was thought to be the sole salvation for women; she was an early supporter of the women's movement; and she chose a Chinese identity during a time when the Chinese were not respected.

When working in a small midwestern town, Sui Sin Far overheard her employer saying:

A Chinaman is, in my eyes, more repulsive than a nigger. . . . Now the Japanese are different altogether. There is something bright and likeable about those men.[11]

The American attitude toward both Chinese-Americans and African-Americans is implied, giving both the same social status, with the African-American perhaps a little higher. According to Sin Far's employer, of the three groups—Chinese-American, African-American, and Japanese-American—Japanese-Americans are superior.

Perhaps this more favorable attitude toward the Japanese prompted Sui Sin Far's sister, Winnifred Eaton (1877–1954), to choose a Japanese persona when Winnifred decided to begin her writing career. Japan was becoming a world power with its defeat of China in 1895 and Russia in 1905, and for the vast majority of the American public, knowledge of China and the Chinese was limited to chinoiserie and the images that existed in popular culture. But there was more pervasive, although superficial, knowledge of the Japanese. Sui Sin Far confirms this standpoint in her memoir.

The Americans having for many years manifested a much higher regard for the Japanese than the Chinese, several half-Chinese young men and women, thinking to advance themselves . . . pass as Japanese. They continue to be known as Eurasian, but a Japanese Eurasian does not appear in the same light as a Chinese Eurasian.[12]

From the opening of Japan to the West by Matthew Perry, the European and American public had been fascinated by Japan. Gilbert and Sullivan's *The Mikado* and other theatrical successes, such as *The Geisha*, *The Mayor of Tokyo*, and Puccini's *Madame Butterfly*, had great influence on the American perception of the Japanese.[13] The reasons for the American appreciation for the Japanese are no doubt complex. However, primarily the images of the Chinese were derived from the fact that many Chinese were present in the United States and the Japanese were still across the Pacific. Thus, it is not surprising that Winnifred Eaton resolved to present herself as a Japanese Eurasian. Although Chinese-American, Winnifred Eaton is outside the scope of this work because she used Japanese themes. But as the first Chinese-American woman novelist, she remains a significant part of Asian-American feminist literature.

As Onoto Watanna, Winnifred Eaton supported herself and her four children by exploiting and possibly confirming prevalent racist and sexist stereotypes in very successful popular fiction and nonfiction[14] from 1901 to 1916. From 1924 to 1931 she wrote and edited movie scripts in Hollywood, eventually becoming director of Universal Studios' scenario department.

Nine years before the death of Winnifred Eaton, Jade Snow Wong published *Fifth Chinese Daughter* (1950), an autobiography. "There is nothing wrong with autobiography," writes Kai-yu Hsu in his introduction to *Asian-American Authors*, "except when one realizes that the perceptions of reality revealed through these works seem to continue to confirm rather than to modify a stereotyped image of the Chinese and their culture."[15]

Wong's life resembles a Horatio Alger story. By hard work and fierce ambition, she overcame her dire financial straits, her ethnicity, and its accompanying traditions to graduate with honors from Mills College. Eventually she established her own very successful ceramics shop in San Francisco's Chinatown, but as Bruce Iwasaki points out in comparing her autobiography to that of Daniel Inouye (*Journey to Washington*, 1967), her story is a myth.

They are also myths when taken as a realistic response to a racist society . . . both writers are fully conscious of the discrimination they have encountered. However, the implicit message . . . is that by succeeding in terms of the majority culture's norms, a sort of victory over racism can be won.[16]

From a 1990s perspective, Jade Snow Wong seems curiously outmoded, but in 1945 it was the prevailing custom to publish patriotic Chinese-Americans who were actually writing thinly disguised anti-Japanese propaganda. After the bombing of Pearl Harbor in 1941, Japanese-Americans became the "bad" Asians, elevating Chinese-Americans to the status of "good" Asians. To disseminate this new perspective of Chinese-Americans, many publishing houses began to publish Chinese-American autobiographies. Frank Chin has no doubts that *Fifth Chinese Daughter* "fits the propaganda-as-autobiography mold perfectly."[17] Many of the chapters were revisions of college essays written during World War II. Certainly the author perpetuates the stereotypical view of the Chinese by presenting them as unassimilated, exotic, misogynist foreigners who have preserved their traditional culture in San Francisco's Chinatown. Demonstrating the hold that the concept of the dual personality has on Chinese-Americans, she writes in the third person because the submergence of the individual is a necessary ingredient of Chinese culture.

In response to exclusion from the majority culture, many Asian-Americans tended to identify more forcefully with Asia. Through this strong identification with China, many Chinese-American women writers became what Mary V. Dearborn[18] refers to as mediators, promoting understanding by working between two cultures. Wong assumes the role of an anthropologist's native informant in her descriptions of shopping for Chinese groceries, rice washing, recipes, festivals, and filial relationships in an attempt to inform her non-Chinese reading public of the lives of a "real" Chinese-American family.

Within this family, Wong, as a female, was continually reminded by her relatives, friends, and neighbors of her insignificance. There were great family celebrations upon the birth of a son but no celebrations for the birth of a daughter. Even at a wedding, "The bride was merely a sort of decorative, noneating, nondrinking, nonspeaking accessory to the wedding celebration"(144). Apparently Wong accepts Chinese sexism as dispassionately as she later accepts Euro-American racism.

Wong's response to discrimination is to fall back upon her "superior" Chinese culture. Once, a classmate, Richard, refers to her with the derogatory epithet, "Chinky." Wong's response is to think of the accomplishments of the Chinese. Thinking of the achievements of her ethnic group rather than becoming angry because of the racial insult demonstrates remarkable "Oriental" control.

Racial insults, although more subtle, continued when Wong was seeking employment, although she seemed to be unaware of them. One of her first jobs was as a servant in the dean's home at Mills College. There she became similar to Sui Sin Far's Mrs. Spring Fragrance, a nonthreatening pet, but Wong feels grateful for being placed on an equal footing with the household animals.

Later, in seeking further employment, she found that her choice of positions was limited by her race. The employment counselor at Mills College informed her that she should seek a position only among the Chinese. Despite the advice, she obtained work as a secretary in the San Francisco naval yards. Unable to decide whether she should continue working there or apply to graduate school, she asked her new boss what he thought. He reminded her that she was a woman and Chinese, and as such her options were limited.

She accepted his advice unquestioningly and began to look for an occupation in which her gender or ethnicity would not be a handicap. She decided to become a potter, an occupation inconsistent with traditional Chinese feminine behavior: Chinese-American women do not open their own businesses and succeed at them.

Early in the book Wong recalls that one of her friends tells her, "But no matter how successful you may become never forget the fight you must make for racial equality. When an individual from a minority group personally succeeds, he too often turns his back on his own group"(153). Jade Snow Wong took that advice to heart and never turned her back on her ethnic group. She became aggressively Chinese, traveling throughout Asia on State Department-sponsored tours attempting to dispel beliefs of the United States' anti-Asian sentiments.

Yet in *Fifth Chinese Daughter* and in her second book, *No Chinese Stranger* (1975), she seems to accommodate the stereotypes of Chinese-Americans as both exotic and the model minority. In her preoccupation with recipes for authentic Chinese dishes, descriptions of festivals, kite making, and traditions such as female submissiveness, she seemingly confirms the Euro-American stereotype of Chinese-Americans.

Certain aspects of Jade Snow Wong's autobiography are incorporated and extended in Virginia Chin-lan Lee's pseudo-autobiography, *The House That Tai Ming Built* (1963). Lee, a fourth-generation American, was born in San Francisco in 1923. Set in San Francisco during World War II, the first section of the book is a retelling of a Chinese legend, "the house that Tai Ming built." Here, Lee glorifies the vitality and beauty of Chinese porcelain, bronzes, and jade. Her use of jade imagery to represent Chinese identity is overworked to the point of caricature.[19] In the manner of other

Chinese-American writers,[20] Lee gives her readers a history lesson that portrays all aspects of Chinese culture as superior.

The plot is remarkably simple. After the extolling of the virtues of Chinese culture in part one, parts two and three are concerned with girl meeting boy and girl losing boy. Both families are opposed to the marriage of Bo Lin Kwong and Scott Hayes. The law forbids their marriage in California, so they decide to elope to Nevada, where interracial marriages are legal. On the day of the planned elopement, Bo Lin receives a telegram informing her of the death of her brother. Unable to marry because of her grief, she says goodbye to Scott, who goes off to war and is killed.

Despite all her love and knowledge of Chinese art and history, Lee's heroine, Bo Lin, is filled with self-loathing because of her ethnicity. After falling in love with Scott and facing rejection from his family and the law, she laments, "Lin Kwong . . . Lin Kwong . . . I wish I had been born an O'Malley, or a Smith"(191).

Like Jade Snow Wong, Lee wishes to explain to her non-Chinese reading audience the superiority of Chinese culture. She relies heavily on research by British and Euro-American historians in a misguided attempt to convince the reader that an idealized seventeenth-century Chinese culture exists in twentieth-century San Francisco's Chinatown.

Throughout the 1940s, 1950s, and 1960s, some Chinese-American writers continued to capitalize on their ethnicity for a non-Asian reading audience. One writer who broke somewhat with this tradition was Diana Chang.

Diana Chang, novelist, poet, and essayist, was born in New York and grew up in Shanghai during World War II. Her first novel, *The Frontiers of Love* (1956), is her only long work of fiction that features Chinese characters. In her other five novels,[21] she has used Euro-Americans as protagonists, seemingly disclaiming her ethnicity.

Chang asserts that, although Eurasian, she does not think of herself as marginal. She is very sure of who she is. However, a possible explanation for her paucity of Asian portrayals is offered by Amy Ling:

"Exoticism" can stand in the way of the "universal" which she strives for in her themes, and therefore she's often subsumed aspects of her background in the interests of other truths. If she writes of white Protestant Americans in *Eye to Eye*, it is because she believes that her theme—creativity—would have been side-tracked had she—writing and publishing—used Chinese, Chicano or Norwegian characters.[22]

However, it is in *The Frontiers of Love* that she explores her ethnicity through the three main characters, who are Eurasian. Feng Hueng (Farthington) is the son of a Chinese father and English mother. He hates the part of himself that is English and eventually joins the Communist party to prevent the further colonization of China. Mimi Lambert, the daughter of a Chinese mother and Australian father, is partial to the Australian half of her ethnicity. After becoming pregnant and then rejected by her Swiss lover, she becomes virulently anti-Chinese. The third is Sylvia Chen, the most balanced of the three characters.

Sylvia, the daughter of a Chinese father who was educated at the University of Missouri and an American mother, "was both as American as her own mother and as Chinese as her father . . . and her exoticness lay in the truth that [she] seemed to have no racial identity at all."[23] She was "uncomfortable in the United States partly because . . . her mother's America was an illusion and was, for her at least, untrue"(50). Nothing in the United States seemed to have a history, especially in New York's Chinatown, where her alienation was even stronger. She "could not even bear to think of it to this day, that ghetto begging tourists to inspect its shame"(490). In the United States, she was ashamed of being Chinese, and in China the shame remained.

She returned from her visit to the United States to Shanghai, where she lives in the foreign section and where she maintains all her ties, never having visited the Chinese parts of the city. Although she is a part of the social life of the Westerners, she feels an animosity toward the foreigners and their colonial mentality. Sylvia seems to apply this bitterness toward most Westerners. While she tries to become a balanced blend of both parents, she seems to realize that the laws and attitudes cause her to be Chinese.

Sylvia is contrasted with another female character, Miss Chu, the schizophrenic Chinese girl with the platinum blond hair who has become imbued with Western culture acquired mostly from movies. Miss Chu's behavior contradicts traditional conduct for middle-class Chinese women. The defiance of tradition is caricatured in Miss Chu but is more evenly balanced in Mimi Lambert, whose mother and aunt had openly defied Chinese tradition. Rosalind Hong, Mimi's mother, had been educated in Paris, where she had picked up free love, democratic ideas, feminism, and bobbed hair.

Rosalind had married a foreigner, an Australian. This is what was expected of her because of her Western education. A tradition-bound Chinese husband would not have accepted her behavior, and she would have had to justify her choice of a Chinese husband to her friends. Their daughter, Mimi, is in the position of belonging to neither group and in competing with her mother and her aunt in their flamboyance.

After her parents are killed in a Japanese bombing raid on Shanghai, Mimi goes to live with her aunt, Juliet, with whom her life becomes a round of society parties. At one of these parties she meets the man who becomes her lover, Robert, a Swiss national. She becomes pregnant, and Robert insists on an abortion, which she refuses. She wants marriage, but he will not marry her because she is Eurasian. Finally understanding, Mimi becomes furious and numb and then spontaneously aborts. She is unable to be at home in a racial climate where she is unacceptable as a wife because she is Eurasian but acceptable as a mistress for the same reason. Afterward she is filled with such self-hatred that she becomes indiscriminate in her choice of lovers, usually choosing an American who, she thinks, can offer her a way out of China.

Diana Chang suggests that the absence of values, traditions, or standards leaves Mimi adrift. Without such values, Mimi becomes confused, immoral, and alienated. The old traditions doubtlessly served a purpose in pre–World War II China, but during the war when traditions were cast aside, there was nothing to replace them. However, although traditions seemed to have been discarded, the position of women remained virtually unchanged.

The weakness and misfortune of women become equated with the misfortunc of Eurasians. Feng Hueng becomes a communist and a murderer, killing Sylvia's cousin, and Mimi becomes promiscuous. Shirley Geok-lin Lim suggests that their tragedies are caused by a lack of "racial belonging."

Sylvia escapes self-destruction, for in her absence of narrow commitment to race is her capacity for enlargement of point-of-view. Aware of her dual selves, she is unwilling to sacrifice one for the other; aware of the individual's vulnerability in search for self-definition, she is capable of objectivity. Her search for point-of-view is finally more authentic than a single comforting bias.[24]

While Lim's point is well taken, the three characters are well aware of their racial designation. It would appear that only monoracial (principally European and Euro-American) persons would equate biraciality with a lack of racial belonging. Mixed race persons are routinely assigned to the "subordinate" group; mulattoes and quadroons are African-American. Although Chang's Eurasians do differ markedly from Eurasians in Anglo-American fiction who have an inner war raging within them, ultimately

Eurasians, similar to mulattas, must decide to accept their "Chineseness" or die.[25]

This ambivalence concerning ethnicity or even gender becomes more apparent in Chuang Hua's first novel, *Crossings* (1968, 1986). Chuang Hua, the daughter of a surgeon, came to the United States as a small child. In this short novel, Chuang Hua experiments with form and structure, reality and fantasy, myth and legend. The work requires close reading; there are few quotation marks, many fragments and run-on sentences, and many unnamed characters. The narration does not proceed geographically or chronologically but rather crosses time erratically, sometimes within the same paragraph.

Briefly, it is the story of a young émigrée Chinese-American woman in Paris and the beginning and the end of her affair with an unnamed married French journalist. Fourth Jane, so named because she is the middle child of a well-to-do family, "First Nancy Chen-Hua, Second Katherine Kwang-Hua, Third Christine Tsawi-Hua, Fourth Jane Chuang-Hua [the author] belonging in name both to the male attribute and the female."[26] *Chuang* is the name given to the boys of the family and *Hua* to the girls. Even in her name there is a crossing or blending of gender.

She has also experienced many geographical crossings. As a child, her parents took her from China to England and then to the United States. As an adult, she decides to move to France. In total, there are seven crossings of the ocean and the concomitant cultural changes that such moves require. Her parents have a close-knit, loving relationship that helps her and the other children ease their sense of displacement. But after Fifth James marries a "barbarian," a Caucasian, tension disrupts their normally affectionate and supportive family relationship. Fourth Jane sides with her parents in their rejection of Fifth James' choice of a spouse. She has a loathing for this woman, yet she never seems to realize the inconsistency of her own taking a French lover. She, too, is intimately involved with a "barbarian."

Parallel to the tension surrounding her brother's marriage is the tension between the two parts of her ethnic identity: American and Chinese. When she first meets her lover-to-be on a Parisian street, he wonders if she is Chinese or American. She herself is unsure. However, he readily assigns the stereotyped image of Chinese women, including infinite patience, to her, but she is unsuccessful at counteracting his beliefs.

Her "Chineseness" becomes a source of constant questioning on the part of her lover. Later in the narrative, he unexpectedly tells her that she should return to China because she is Chinese and not American. But she eventually decides that she can be both Chinese and American without losing her sense of self. She concludes that China and the United States have fused within her. "I can't separate any more. If I were to live in China today I would have to conceal one half of myself. In America I need not hide what I am" (125).

She resolves the conflict between her two cultural identities, but her gender presents a less easily resolved dilemma. She strives to liberate herself from learned feminine social responses. She remembers a ghost tale told to her by an amah (nurse):

Formerly the condemned were dressed in red on their way to execution. Brides also wear red on their wedding day just like criminals and like bride mouse in the comic strip stepping out of her curtained palanquin to be greeted at the entrance of her future home by groom mouse and attendant mice. Her dress is red though her veil and wreath are white. No, no not Mickey Mouse and Minnie Mouse, this is the story of Chinese mice. (45)

Women about to be married are compared to convicts about to be executed. Chuang Hua seems to share the attitudes of Larsen and Walker that marriage is an unnatural state for women, analogous to a living death involving a loss of identity and, in a sense, personhood. Marriage becomes for them a giving up of life and self-identity in order to become a zombie who neither thinks nor makes decisions. Rather, she becomes a creature who cooks and cleans and, in traditional Chinese culture, is a servant to her in-laws, particularly the mother-in-law.

Even after becoming pregnant by her lover, she does not consider marriage, perhaps in an effort to avoid becoming like her mother, who

plays her primal biological role, bearing one child after another and with fierce stubbornness wards off life's decorations and pretensions unafflicted and disregarding ambition not related to the producing and caring of children, withdrawing to an out of the way hole in the world like a rabbit burrowed in a dark tunnel.(177)

Mice and rabbits seem like curious images to use in relation to women, but in traditional Chinese culture, the rabbit symbolizes fecundity and the mouse is associated with evil. Are women in their traditional roles as wives and mothers causing harm to themselves and to others by devoting their time and energy solely to their children? Women as mice and rabbits are quiet and timid, not daring to disobey the dictates of society. Desiring to be neither a mouse nor a rabbit, she never informs her lover of her pregnancy. Instead she packs and leaves Paris.

Fourth Jane is a very complex woman who searches within herself in an effort to create an Asian-American feminist sensibility. She considers herself an outsider in China, the United States, and France. By choosing not to marry, she becomes an outsider in another way. Marriage as a convention ostracizes those who do not follow the rules.

Fourth Jane is very much a contemporary woman, quite unlike the woman that Amy Ling describes as ethnically confused. She appears to be an ethnically secure, determined person who makes her own decisions and does not succumb to traditional determinants. For example, she spurns her father's marriage choice. After becoming pregnant by her lover, she decides to leave Paris in order to give birth without his knowledge. She makes choices rather than allowing traditions to decide for her. She makes her decisions by taking from both of her ethnic heritages. By interweaving the myths and traditions of China with those of the West and by combining the feminine behaviors of both groups, Chuang Hua creates a woman who is a combination of both. She creates a person who is unique—not Chinese and not American but Chinese-American.

Following the tradition of Chuang Hua in the use of myth and legend to create new literary forms is Maxine Hong Kingston. She, too, writes of being Chinese in the United States but from a perspective different from that of earlier writers. Kingston's implicit intent is to explore her individual identity in addition to her ethnicity. In her use of myth and legend in an attempt to create a Chinese-American feminist sensibility, she is closely allied to Chuang Hua.

In *The Woman Warrior. Memoirs of a Childhood among Ghosts* (1977), Kingston undertakes to challenge the prevailing Chinese-American beliefs about women and define herself ethnically, that is, literally to invent herself. She wants to demonstrate that being Chinese-American is not the same as being Chinese in America. Further, she wishes to determine her place within her community, a community that traditionally has devalued women.

With her first tale, she is cautioned that the responsibility of being a woman is onerous. And because she is a woman, she must obey the male-sanctioned traditions. As Zhang Ya-ji, a professor of American literature in China, writes about life for women in China, "if anything happens or even nothing happens but just gossip, the blame usually falls on the woman."[27] Kingston's mother, Brave Orchid, confirms this assessment through the use of scare tactics to impose a continuation of traditions. Brave Orchid tells her the story of her aunt, No-name Woman, so called because she broke the communal injunctions against adultery. As punishment for her behavior, the village acted as one in the destruction of the family's property. After the birth of her baby, No-name Woman drowned herself and her baby in the family well. Brave Orchid's tale is intended to warn her daughter of the consequences of opposing male-ordered traditions. Like Alice Walker's Celie in *The Color Purple*, silence is imposed on Kingston.

The tale of the No-name Woman serves to testify "to the power of the patriarchy to command through mothers the silence of daughters, to name and to unname them and thereby to control their meaning in discourse itself."[28] Through the male prerogative to include women in the process, women countenance their own oppression.

Kingston writes that "we failed if we grew up to be but wives or slaves" (24), the only options allowed Chinese women. This statement is followed by the story of Fa Mu Lan in "White Tigers." Fa Mu Lan, the woman warrior, goes up the mountain to acquire physical and spiritual strength in order to avenge her village. After defeating the village's enemies, she returns home not as a mere woman but as an exceptional woman, that is, a man. "My parents killed a chicken . . . as if they were welcoming home a son" (40). No more is expected of her; she returns to her original position as the traditional daughter-in-law. She tells them, "I will stay with you, doing farmwork and housework, and giving you more sons" (54). Fa Mu Lan is acceptable only when disguised as a man; regaining her true identity, she must once more be subservient. A woman fails if she is not a wife or slave.

The sayings of her childhood remind Kingston of her subordination: "Girls are maggots in the rice. It is more profitable to raise geese than daughters" (51). "Feeding girls is feeding cowbirds" (54). "When you raise girls, you're raising children for strangers" (54).[29] The language continually reminds her of her insignificance. "There is a Chinese word for the female I—which is 'slave' " (56). The sayings, the language, the ambiguity of the tale that emphasizes woman as wife, slave, and warrior compel Kingston to become a "bad girl." And like Toni Morrison's Sula, she decides, "Isn't a bad girl almost a boy?" (56). She refuses to participate in any of the traditional female duties. She earns straight A's and refuses to learn to cook. If she has to wash dishes, she "would crack one or two"(56). In short, she assumes "the cultural postures of male selfhood. . . . [But her efforts] to be the phallic woman do not earn the love and acceptance of her mother and community, as they do Fa Mu Lan."[30]

These first two stories are Kingston's expansion and enhancement of her mother's tales, but the third is of the mother herself. Brave Orchid is a woman warrior; she has left the comfort and familiarity of China for a new adventure in the United States.

After her husband's departure for the United States and the deaths of her first two children, Brave Orchid returns to school and becomes a doctor. She is very successful, as she only chooses patients who she thinks will survive. But when her husband has saved enough money for her to join him in the United States, she leaves her privileged life and very lucrative practice to work in the family laundry and in the fruit and vegetable fields outside Compton, California.

Brave Orchid survives, perhaps, as a result of resorting to the survival tactics that were developed against the discriminatory immigration policies of the United States. (Kingston later develops the theme in *China Men*.) Moon Orchid, Brave Orchid's sister with whom she is contrasted, is not as fortunate.

As was prevalent during the period when the Chinese were considered sojourners, Moon Orchid's husband had left her in China while he immigrated to the United States. He became a successful neurosurgeon and had remarried though continuing to support her. Brave Orchid continually pressures Moon Orchid to confront her (Moon Orchid's) husband, who is unnamed. When Moon Orchid vacillates, Brave Orchid reminds her of the Chinese custom of dealing with the second wife. The first wife has priority over the second wife; therefore, the first wife can move into the husband's home and take over, as in Frank Chin's *The Year of the Dragon*. The second wife literally becomes the slave of the first. Despite this custom, however, the debonair, Americanized husband rejects Moon Orchid's claim, which eventually leads to her madness and death.

Where Brave Orchid is fearless, successful, intelligent, and heroic, Moon Orchid is weak, delicate, elegant, and decorative. In her attempts to preserve traditional Chinese culture within an American environment, Brave Orchid succeeds only in making other women unhappy. Moon Orchid is institutionalized, and Moon Orchid's daughter is locked into an unhappy marriage arranged by Brave Orchid.

Kingston suggests that not all women can successfully negotiate a foreign environment. Each woman must choose her own strategies for survival, as did Kingston's grandfather's third wife who was African. Kingston acknowledges, albeit tacitly, the historical attempt to negroicize Chinese-Americans.

In the last tale, "A Song for a Barbarian Reed Pipe," she makes her position on mother-daughter relationships clearer. The second-century poetess Ts'ai Yen represents both Kingston and Brave Orchid.

Ts'ai Yen was captured and carried off by an invading tribe whose language and culture she did not understand. She eventually had two children, who did not speak her language. Neither did she communicate well with the barbarians. Ts'ai Yen thought that this nomadic tribe had only the death sounds of their arrows for music until one night she heard their flutes struggling to reach a high note.

The story of Ts'ai Yen becomes the story of Brave Orchid, who is "ringed by barbarians" in the United States. She cannot speak the language or understand the culture of the barbarians or her children. Furthermore, she can communicate with her daughter only through her "talk-stories." Yet, somehow, as Ts'ai Yen's children do, Kingston does understand and ultimately identify with her mother.

Kingston's act of self-definition becomes doubly important when it is understood that she and other ethnic writers of color must overcome

those publishers and critics who consistently reject any writings contradicting popular racist views of Asian-Americans as either totally exotic, as no different from anyone else (denial of culture), or, finally as model minorities (humble, well-mannered, law abiding, family-oriented, hard-working, education seeking.)[31]

Kingston not only had to overcome the Euro-American publishers and critics but also Chinese-American male critics. Critics like Frank Chin and Benjamin Tong have attacked Kingston, just as African-American male critics attacked Walker's *The Color Purple*. Chin and Tong have accused Kingston of exoticizing her ethnicity and demonstrating an antimale bias in order to appeal to a Euro-American reading audience. However, a close reading of *The Woman Warrior* or her second work, *China Men*, clearly reveals her need to understand what it means to be not only Chinese-American but also a Chinese-American woman.

In her redefining of herself, Kingston resorts to a reinterpretation of a mixture of Chinese myths and legends, which she retells from an American perspective, thereby firmly establishing her American identity. Within this identity she acknowledges the racial stereotypes surrounding the Chinese and strives to dissociate herself from them. One of these preconceptions is the quiet, submissive Chinese woman, which she perceives as a response to a racist environment. Kingston conquers her speechlessness through the use of the English language to wed her Chinese past to her American present, creating an American identity that is neither explicitly Chinese nor white American.

In *The Woman Warrior*, usually assumed to be an autobiographical[32] work, Kingston focused on her mother and their relationship. Amy Tan, in *The Joy Luck Club*, focuses on four Chinese mothers and their Chinese-American daughters.

In 1943 President Franklin D. Roosevelt repealed the Exclusion Act, which had been renewed in 1904. With the repeal, 105 Chinese a year were allowed into the United States, and Chinese immigrants gained the right of naturalization. The War Brides Act of 1945 and the Fiancées Act of 1946 subsequently allowed the wives and fiancées of servicemen to enter the country; they were not charged against the quota of 105. Afterward Congress passed a separate bill that allowed the wives and children of Chinese-Americans to apply for entry as "nonquota" immigrants. Supposedly from this group of women came the mothers in *The Joy Luck Club*. Tan mentions none of this history, nor should she. However, Tan leaves the reader with the impression that Chinese immigrant history is no different from European immigrant history.

The title refers to a club of four older, émigrée Chinese women who meet regularly at one another's homes in San Francisco to play mah-jongg,[33] buy stocks, cook, and gossip. The death of one of them, Suyuan Woo, leaves a vacancy, and Jing-mei, or June, her thirty-six-year-old daughter, takes her place. At June's first meeting, the three older Chinese women tell her of her mother's first two daughters, who were abandoned during World War II. They explain to June that she must go to China, meet the daughters, and explain her mother to them. This remembrance of a mother and a friend touches off a series of stories, told by each of the mothers and their Chinese-American daughters.

As in Kingston's *The Woman Warrior* and the works of many African-American women writers, male-female relationships have less importance than the relationships between mother and daughter. These mother-daughter relationships are very strong, on the one hand, because of love and respect but, on the other hand, are weak because of ethnic and generational conflicts. The mothers expect their daughters to have the characteristics of American women, such as strength, drive, and success, while maintaining the subservience and conformity of traditional Chinese women.

The mythical Chinese character and way of thinking is unveiled in the stories of the four mothers. In the first of these, An-mei Hsu watched her mother, a concubine, commit suicide. The mother had been ostracized by her family when she decided (under pressure) to become the fourth wife of wealthy Wu Tsing. Chinese widows are not to remarry. But the second mother, Suyuan Woo, remarried after her husband died fighting the Japanese. While escaping the Japanese, she left two babies on the road. It is these twin baby girls whom her daughter, June, is supposed to meet in China. The third mother, Lindo Jong, escaped an arranged marriage and through cunning and intelligence emigrated to the United States. She satisfied immigration authorities by pretending to be a prospective theology student. The fourth mother, Ying-ying St. Clair, is abandoned by her rich, profligate husband and very shrewdly meets a Euro-American visiting China. She marries him and goes to live with him in California. The four stories of the mothers are a testament to the strength and resilience of women.

The daughters are not as strong as the mothers; neither are they as remarkable, though each of the daughters has achieved some measure of American success. Waverly Jong becomes a junior chess champion and a successful tax attorney. Rose Hsu Jordan is a graphic artist who is coping unsuccessfully with a deteriorating marriage. Lena St. Clair is an architect who is also dealing with a bad marriage and living in a rehabbed barn. And Jing-mei Woo, who is introduced at the beginning of the novel, is an advertising copywriter, not as successful as the others.

The novel is more than a listing of accomplishments and stories. Like much of the writing by African-American women, it is about female relationships. Each mother has hopes and dreams and fears for her daughter. The trepidation that the mothers feel is always a part of their consciousness. Their daughters are not always aware of the hopes and fears that the mothers brought to the United States. However, the daughters, although born in the United States and culturally American, are not significantly different from their mothers.

As the mothers have journeyed from China to the United States, the daughters too must journey, but the daughters are seeking to find themselves. Because the mothers have influenced them, shaped them, loved them, and created them, in finding themselves, they find that they are like their mothers.

The majority of Chinese-American women writers like Amy Tan set the majority of their writings in China or in a mythical Chinatown where supposedly seventeenth-century aristocratic Chinese culture still exists. They staunchly emphasize their "Chineseness" as opposed to their "Americanness" or "Chinese-Americanness." With their stress on all the components of Chinese culture, they make the myth of the dual personality credible. But Han Suyin, the Hong Kong Chinese author of eight novels, including *Love Is a Many Splendored Thing*, has written, "These books [are] lauded as 'authentic' when they are only tasty rehash of what pleases ingrained prejudices."[34] An exception, though somewhat historically inaccurate, to this pattern is Ruthanne Lum McCunn's *Thousand Pieces of Gold*, a biography of Lalu Nathoy (1853—1933), who was abducted in China and sold as a slave in the United States. Through thrift and hard work, she subsequently became a respected property owner in Idaho, an early example of the stereotype of the model minority. Still, most of these writers ignore their popular culture images or history in the United States, preferring instead to reinforce their identification with China.

NOTES

1. Elaine Kim, "Visions and Fierce Dreams: A Commentary on the Works of Maxine Hong Kingston," *MELUS* 8:2 (1981): 145–61.

2. Ibid.

3. *New York Times* (April 19, 1914): 11.

4. Sui Sin Far, "Leaves from the Mental Portfolio of an Eurasian," *Independent* 66 (January 7, 1909): 127.

5. Frank Chin et al., eds., *AAIIIEEEE. An Anthology of Asian-American Writers* (Washington, D.C., 1983), xxi–xxii.

6. S. E. Solberg, "Sui Sin Far/Edith Eaton: First Chinese American Fictionist," *MELUS* 8:1 (1981): 33.

7. *New York Times* (July 7, 1912): 405.

8. Lorraine Dong and Marlon K. Hom, "Defiance or Perpetuation: An Analysis of Characters in *Mrs. Spring Fragrance," Chinese America: History and Perspectives,* 1987 : 48.

9. Sui Sin Far, *Mrs. Spring Fragrance* (Chicago: A. C. McClurg, 1912), 194.

10. Dong and Hom, 148.

11. Far, *Independent* 66 (January 7, 1909): 129.

12. Far, "Leaves from the Mental Portfolio of an Eurasian," 131.

13. The Chinese Exclusion Act of 1882 was repeatedly renewed until 1943, after Pearl Harbor dramatically reversed the popular opinions of the Chinese and Japanese.

14. Onoto Watanna, *Cattle* (London: Hutchinson, 1923; New York: W. J. Watt, 1924) *Daughters of Nijo* (New York: Macmillan, 1904); *The Diary of Delia* (Garden City, NY: Doubleday, 1907); *The Heart of the Hyacinth* (New York: Harper, 1903); *His Royal Nibs* (New York: W. J. Watt, 1924); *The Honorable Miss Moonlight* (New York: Harper, 1912); *A Japanese Blossom* (New York: Harper, 1906); *A Japanese Nightingale* (New York: Harper, 1906); *The Love of Azalea* (New York: Dodd, Mead, 1904); *Me, a Book of Remembrance* (New York: Century, 1915); *Marion: A Story of an Artist's Model by Herself and the Author of Me* (New York: W. J. Watt, 1916); *Miss Numè of Japan: A Japanese-American Romance* (Chicago: Rand, McNally, 1899); *Sunny San* (New York: George H. Doran, 1922); *Tama* (New York: Harper, 1910); *The Wooing of Wistaria* (New York: Harper, 1910).

15. Kai-yu Hsu and Helen Palubinskas, eds., *Asian-American Authors* (Boston: Houghton Mifflin Co., 1972), v.

16. Bruce Iwasaki, "Response and Change for the Asian in America. A Survey of Asian American Literature," in *Roots: An Asian American Reader* ed., Amy Tachiki (Los Angeles: UCLA Asian American Studies Center, 1971), 93.

17. Chin et al., xiv.

18. Mary V. Dearborn, *Pocahontas's Daughters. Gender and Ethnicity in American Culture* (New York: Oxford University Press, 1986). Dearborn writes that the writing of ethnic women is heavily weighted toward the family, with an emphasis on female relationships. There is less attention given to the male. He is absolute; she is the other. Thus, the ethnic woman becomes an outsider twice in the United States. She is an outsider in her family because she is not male and an outsider in the dominant culture. Additionally, many ethnic women writers attempt to authenticate themselves through explanations of their culture, usage of glossaries, or annotations and mediation (concept of working between two cultures).

19. Characters drink from jade cups, p. 96; play on jade flutes, p. 97; rouge jars carved in jade, p. 98; jade earrings, p. 112; jade bracelets, p. 126; speak in jade tones, p. 123; her uncle strokes his jade piece, pp. 124, 128; jade amulets, p. 140.

20. Jade Snow Wong's *Fifth Chinese Daughter* and *No Chinese Stranger*; Pardee Lowe, *Father and Glorious Descendant* (Boston: Little, Brown & Co., 1943); Betty Lee Sung, *Mountain of Gold* (New York: Macmillan Co., 1967), and *The Chinese in America* (New York: Macmillan Co., 1972). Gerald Haslam writes on page 80 in *Forgotten Pages of American Literature* (Boston: Houghton Mifflin, 1970),

Yet the average Chinese-American at least knows that China *has* produced "great literatures and philosophies," and with that knowledge has come a greater sense of ethnic pride. Contrasted, for example with the abject cultural deprivation long foisted upon Afro-Americans, Asian-Americans have an inner resource: the knowledge that their ancestors had created a great and complex civilization when the inhabitants of the British Isles still painted their faces blue.

21. *Eye to Eye* (New York: Harper and Row, 1974); *A Passion for Life* (New York: Random House, 1961); *A Perfect Love* (New York: Jove, 1978); *The Only Game in Town* (New York: Signet, 1963); *A Woman of Thirty* (New York: Random House, 1959).

22. Amy Ling, "Writer in the Hyphenated Condition: Diana Chang," *MELUS* 7:4 (1980): 75.

23. Diana Chang, *Frontiers of Love* (New York: Random House, 1956), 19, 12.

24. Shirley Geok-lin Lim, "Twelve Asian American Writers: In Search of Self-Definition," *MELUS* 13:1 (1986): 74.

25. Achmed Abdulla, *The Honourable Gentleman and Other Stories* (New York: Knickerbocker Press, 1919); Rex Beach, *Son of the Gods* (New York: Harper and Brothers, 1929); Frank L. Packard, *The Dragon's Jaws* (Garden City, NY: Crime Club, 1937); Herbert G. Woodworth, *In the Shadow of Lantern Street* (Boston: Small, Maynard and Co., 1920).

26. Chuang Hua, *Crossings* (Boston: Northeastern University Press, 1986, 1968), 31.

27. Ya-jie Zhang, "A Chinese Woman's Response to Maxine Hong Kingston's *The Woman Warrior*," *MELUS* 13:3 (1986): 106.

28. Sidonie Smith, *A Poetics of Women's Autobiography. Marginality and the Fictions of Self-Representation* (Bloomington: Indiana University Press, 1987), 156.

29. Although Kingston writes of the devaluation of women in China, contradictions are inherent in the descriptions of a grandfather who traded his son for a girl.

30. Smith, 160.

31. Paul John Eakins, *Fictions in Autobiography. Studies in the Art of Self-Invention* (Princeton, NJ: Princeton University Press, 1985), 165.

32. Kingston originally intended for her work to be published as a novel, but her publishers convinced her that the work would sell better as autobiography.

33. A game of Chinese origin usually played by four persons with 144 domino-like tiles marked in suits, counters, and dice, the object being to build a winning combination of pieces.

34. Han Suyin in *Between Worlds. Women Writers of Chinese Ancestry* (New York: Pergamon Press, 1990), x.

Chapter Six

African-Americans and Chinese-Americans

African-American women and Chinese-American women have had a similar history in the United States. Both are visible minorities with similar reputations. Among the many similarities, both have been accused of immorality, as well as of lacking affection for their children.

A literary stereotype is a reproduction of an earlier literary image without significant creative change or originality. Character analysis of a stereotype is needless since both the writer and the reader subconsciously concur on the significance of physical qualities, personality traits, behaviors, and even speech patterns. These characteristics are predetermined by the stereotype. The three definitions (printing, sociological, and literary) eliminate the need to think or make decisions about a piece of copy, a group or a character. Because conclusions have already been drawn, the stereotyper is able to rationalize the hostility he or she feels toward the stereotyped group. The rationalization allows the stereotyper to justify the violence and oppression directed toward the out-group. A writer does not have to create fully developed characters, but can rely on previous portrayals that allow the reader to predict behaviors.

For the stereotypers, or members of the in-group, the stereotype functions in various ways. Primarily, stereotyping is a social control mechanism providing justification of the treatment of the outsiders, allowing the outsiders to be exploited and keeping them powerless. Stereotyping provides simplistic solutions to complex problems, gives order to the stereotyper's universe, promotes a sense of social solidarity and racial superiority, and provides group cohesiveness as the in-group shares a common view of the outsider, thus sustaining a specific social, political, and literary culture. These views of the out-group are validated in popular fiction because few writers have ventured outside previously established parameters.

The use of ethnic or racial stereotypes is not limited to the dominant group. Minority groups maintain stereotypes of the majority group. However, since these images arise from what is essentially a powerless group, they are not as forceful or influential as those stereotypes emanating from the dominant group. Racially specific beliefs held by an out-group cannot circumscribe or distort the existence of the dominant group. Therefore, stereotypes that originate in the subordinate group have little effect. Stereotypes are, however, very powerful, causing the stereotyper to feel superior and, at the same time, assigning those who are stereotyped to an inferior position. That position is usually reserved for ethnics of color. Ethnic stereotypes, those distorted representations or characteristics, assist in the segregation, exclusion, and definition of the stereotyped group.

In the United States, ethnics of color customarily have been placed in an inferior position socially, morally, and culturally. African-Americans were assigned this inferior position to justify their enslavement. Racial theories developed around their alleged inferiority, and these theories were further disseminated in fiction. As a result, many Euro-American authors did not find it necessary to develop authentic African-American, or Chinese-American, women characters because through the use of stereotyped characters, they provided readers with immediate predictability of the behavior or morality of the character.

However, it seems that women of color can be categorized in this manner since they have been consistently characterized through their sexuality. For example, Hispanic women are stereotyped as sultry, hot, and easily aroused and Native American women as savage and degenerate. *Squaw*, the word commonly used to describe Native American women, is from the Algonquin for "vagina." Their sexuality or their alleged looseness has been used to keep them in a different caste. The degraded images of women of color were used to reinforce the assumed purity and virtue of Euro-American women while at the same time controlling them. Euro-American women were expected to achieve an almost unattainable level of morality, while an inappreciable morality was granted to some women of color. This placement separated the groups of women into "good" and "bad" and had power and control as its aim. The lack of solidarity among American women is reflected in the general acceptance of the stereotypes assigned each group. Many of the sexual allegations surrounding women of color, and implicitly all women, were conceived by Euro-American men, seemingly to satisfy some need. It must not be overlooked that part of the stereotype surrounding women of color is concerned with the love and respect that these women have for Euro-American men. This ego-building process promotes their own desirability and masculinity by insisting that they are loved and desired by all women. This belief, along with others, became an integral part of the stereotype encompassing women of color.

Consequently, the conventional depictions of African-American women in American fiction can be placed into four categories: the tragic mulatta; Aunt Jemima or mammy; the "loose" woman; and the relatively recent, media-created Sapphire. Each preconception serves to substantiate the inferiority and difference of the African-American woman in comparison to the Euro-American woman. Euro-American women were romanticized as perfect mothers who were above all sexually pure. Since slave women allegedly were not sexually pure and did not love their children, they were not "good" women, and their children could be sold to maximize the owner's profits. Chinese mothers, too, according to the stereotype, did not love their children, especially their daughters, on whom they presumably practiced infanticide or sold.

The overriding stereotype of Chinese women in the United States was as prostitutes. The alleged immorality of Chinese-Americans was used as one of the arguments for the Chinese Exclusion Act of 1882. This image frequently appeared in the fictional writings of many Euro-Americans, where they were presented as exotic Chinatown attractions, along with gambling and drugs. However, Sui Sin Far seems to be the only Chinese-American woman writer who used these women in her writings. She depicted these "slave girls" as vain and manipulative. In "Lin John," the girl is quite comfortable in her life as a prostitute, although her brother worked three years to earn the money to buy her freedom, which to her meant poverty. "To have no one to buy me good dinners and pretty things—to be gay no more!" So she stole the money from Lin John, and with it she bought a sealskin coat. The brother vowed that he would work another three years to earn the money again. As he left crestfallen, she whispered, "Fool!"[1]

One of the characteristics of the prostitute was passivity or submissiveness. The assumption was that Chinese prostitutes were meek and unassertive creatures who because of some cultural trait did as they were told. This inaccurate belief has been almost as enduring as the image of the prostitute. The recent acceleration of interest in mail-order brides attests to its longevity. And the image has been reinforced in the writings of many

Chinese-American women who confirmed that they indeed paid obeisance to a patriarchy.

Perhaps the most contradictory portrayal of Chinese-American women is that of the Dragon Lady, the strong, assertive, independent, and incredibly beautiful creation of cartoonist Milton Caniff. In many respects, the Dragon Lady was the opposite of both African-American women and Euro-American women.

Curiously, she is the Dragon *Lady* and not the Dragon Woman. Lady is a term usually reserved for Euro-American women and carries with it certain connotations of "good" family background, social position, and breeding. The word *lady* was not generally applied to African-American women. As Rosalind Miles writes, "It was a well-known fact that a nigger couldn't be a lady . . . every southern gentleman had a library of books by other scientific gentlemen proving that she . . . wasn't even a fully human woman."[2] African-American women and other women of color were *women*, not ladies. The Dragon Lady seems to have been elevated to a quasi-Euro-American level with her designation as lady. The depiction of the Dragon Lady was also different in other respects. She was very curvaceous, elegant, intelligent, ruthless, and the commander of men, which further reinforced the Chinese male stereotype as effeminate. In many ways, she did not conform to the standard stereotype of Chinese and Chinese-American women as compliant, obedient, and submissive or robot-like. She did conform, however, to the stereotyped image of unstinting evil, smoldering sexuality, and the need for a Euro-American male to rescue her from her oppressive cultural tradition. Since the creation of the Dragon Lady, any Chinese-American woman or, indeed any woman, who deviates from the prevailing standard of feminine behavior has been called a Dragon Lady; Imelda Marcos of the Philippines, Madame Nhu of South Vietnam, and Michelle Duvalier of Haiti, among others, have been referred to as Dragon Ladies.

Within certain bounds, the Dragon Lady, like her countrywomen and the African-American woman, was sexually available to Euro-American men. It seems that the African-American woman and the Chinese-American woman were considered sexually available because they did not and could not meet the standards of beauty and morality generally attributed to most Euro-American women. They are not as pink and white (words loaded with positive connotations as opposed to *black* and *yellow*), fresh, delicate, innocent, and inviolable as the Euro-American woman was commonly described. The African-American woman and the Chinese-American woman could be violated with impunity because the former was merely passionate, indiscriminate, and indiscreet, and the latter intrinsically knew how to please a man.

None of the stereotypes of Chinese-American women or of African-American women is positive, although superficially the Aunt Jemima or mammy may appear so. The Aunt Jemima image is rather schizophrenic. The mammy is the nurturing earth mother, providing the only love and affection many Southern Euro-Americans have claimed to have known. Still, she is unlike a Euro-American mother. With her identifying turban and gingham dress, she is very dark, obese, jolly, and lax in her personal hygiene. While the Aunt Jemima usually is not married and yet may have many children, she is not that different from the loose woman, who more often than not is also unmarried with many children.

The "loose" woman may be more amoral than immoral. Her sexuality is innate, extended to any and all who desire her. Her real-life counterpart was created in the antebellum South to increase the number of slaves for the slave owner, and she became, as Toni Morrison states, "property that reproduced itself without cost."[3] If she did not breed, she was soon replaced by slave women who were more fertile. The assumption was that she enjoyed repeated sexual contact, not only with men of her own race but particularly with Euro-American men. A further assumption was that she believed that through these sexual contacts, she would increase her social status. Thus the stereotype justified sexual exploitation or, actually, rape. Inasmuch as this sexual contact could not be consensual, any sexual liaison between a free man and women he owns or controls must inherently be a form of rape. These illicit sexual relationships between the owner and his slave produced mulattas.

The mulatta in American fiction is frequently preceded by the word *tragic* because she supposedly is confused about her identity and because she is victimized. Fiction from the early abolitionists to the 1950s followed certain patterns with slight deviation in its use of the mulatta character. In this basic plot, the mulatta was invariably very beautiful and usually physically indistinguishable from a European. She might have a certain curliness to her hair and an underlying duskiness to the skin, but that was all the racial identification that was visible to the uninitiated. She was well educated and had been socialized as a Euro-American. For different reasons, usually the death of a relative, she discovered her true racial identity. There was turmoil, denial, and finally acceptance, after which she might decide to devote herself to "uplifting" work for the betterment of the race, or she might marry a Euro-American and move abroad, usually to Spain or Italy, where her coloring would not make her suspect.

   The beauty, elegance, and refinement of the mulattas are missing in the Sapphire; she is the antithesis of the mulatta. Sapphire, a media-created stereotype probably originating on the "Amos and Andy" radio program, is not found in fiction to the same extent as the other images. She is an unattractive, strong, loud, bawdy, castrating woman whose identifying characteristics are her hands on her hips and a sharp tongue ready to slash her perceived enemies, usually the African-American male. She can hold her own in any situation, giving as well as she gets. The Sapphire character readily gained widespread popularity with African-American male writers who propagated the myth of the emasculating African-American female.

   Sapphire, tragic mulatta, Aunt Jemima, and the "loose" woman: these are the images (with slight variations) of African-American women in American culture. These images entered fiction in varying forms and became ingrained in the American psyche. For reasons that psychologists will have to provide, Euro-Americans have fabricated and maintained these images for centuries.

   Variations of these images were used in the writing of African-American women, but for a different effect. The writings of African-American women in the beginning were intended to contradict the stereotypes, to demonstrate to their Euro-American reading public that African-American women were no different from them. However, because of a lack of models, writers like Frances Harper and Pauline Hopkins tended to copy the themes, styles, and characters of the Euro-American writers. Therefore, as in many other stereotypical depictions, there are some elements of truth that are not necessarily applicable to all mulattas. A mulatta in the writings of African-Americans is not necessarily tragic but simply is of mixed heritage. A nurturing earth mother similar to the Aunt Jemima stereotype is usually a more complex, fully developed character. Some African-American women writers may even create a very strong, independent woman, as in the Sapphire stereotype, but one who appears strong only within her family, not outside it. In the dominant culture she is once again forced into one of the stereotypical roles.

   The stereotypical characterizations, particularly of the tragic mulatta or mulatta who wished to "pass," to live and be accepted as a Euro-American although possessing some African ancestry, continued with diminishing intensity until Gwendolyn Brooks published *Maude Martha*. The character of Maude Martha is so at variance with previous images of African-American women that the novel has virtually been ignored. *Maude Martha* became the dividing line between the "old" African-American women's writing, which depicted only positive aspects of African-Americans, and the "new," that is, somewhat more authentic. Consequently the publication of *Maude Martha* initiated the development of more honest African-American women characters in real-life situations.

Writers like Marshall, Morrison, and Walker continued in the tradition begun by Brooks and created more authentic female characters. Although African-American women writers have created characters who have persisted in attempting to dispel the traditional images, the contradiction of stereotypes was not their main concern. Rather, they are creating new African-American female characters who question the status quo ethnically and sexually.

The image of African-American women as Aunt Jemima became the requisite image of African-American women for the dominant culture. She became a very powerful symbol that evolved into perhaps the antithesis of Euro-American womanhood, a woman who was dark, obese, and crude. The comparable symbol of Chinese-American women was the accommodating prostitute.

This image no doubt derived in part from the Euro-American image of Chinese women at the end of the nineteenth century. There is some controversy over the identity of the first Chinese woman to arrive in the United States. However, most historians generally agree that the second woman was probably a prostitute, Ah Choi. She differed from later Chinese prostitutes in that she was a "freelancer" who ran her own brothel in San Francisco. The discovery of gold caused many kinds of people to come to California, including prostitutes of various nationalities. But it has been estimated that of the Chinese women in San Francisco's Chinatown in the 1870 census, 71 percent were prostitutes.[4]

The Chinese community was virtually an all-male society since "decent" women were not allowed to immigrate by Chinese authorities nor, with certain exceptions, did the policy of the United States government allow Chinese women to enter the country. Racist laws that prohibited marriages between Chinese men and Euro-American women encouraged prostitution among the Chinese as an alternative to celibacy. Many illegal activities surrounded the arrival of "slave girls" into the United States. These women were bought, kidnapped, or lured into leaving China. In nineteenth-century China, many factors impelled a family to sacrifice an unimportant family member, a daughter, so that an important one, a son, might survive. Once in the United States, some of these women were forced to sign contracts that would keep them enslaved or indentured in perpetuity. Not all of these women were prostitutes; many females, seven to twelve years old, were domestic servants who could be bought, sold, or traded at the whim of the owner. If by chance one of these women, prostitute or servant, escaped from her owner, she married, probably to a

Chinese laborer. Contrary to popular opinion, prostitution was not honorable among the Chinese, but there did not seem to be the same stigma attached to prostitution as there was among Euro-Americans. Apparently prostitutes were generally seen by the Chinese as loyal daughters who obeyed the wishes of the family rather than as "fallen women."

Many of these women had children as a result of their "professional experiences." Lucy Cheng Hirata speculates that the boys were sent to the missions to be educated while the girls remained in the brothels to follow their mothers' profession.[5] These children were among the first Chinese born in the United States, and they should be an important part of Chinese-American history. Significantly, they are missing from most Chinese-American fiction.

Not only are the children of Chinese prostitutes missing in most Chinese-American writing but also missing are the Eurasians, the offspring of a European or Euro-American and an Asian. They were not ignored by Euro-American writers. Writers like Mrs. Lu Wheat (*The Third Daughter: A Story of Chinese Home Life*), Wallace Irwin (*Seed of the Sun*), Sax Rohmer (the Fu Manchu series), Rex Beach (*Son of the Gods*), and others prominently featured Eurasian characters. In this fiction, Eurasians usually exhibited characteristics similar to mulatta characters. They were portrayed as inherently degenerate, beautiful, and tragic in the same sense as mulattas: they could not be European, and they would not be Chinese. Sui Sin Far and Diana Chang seem to be the only Chinese-American women writers who featured Eurasian characters, male or female.

In stark contrast to the lack of Eurasian characters in Chinese-American writing, there is an abundance of mulatta characters in African-American writing. African-American women writers used the mulatta character in an attempt to create new myths that they hoped would dispel those of the dominant culture. Also many felt that their primarily Euro-American reading audience would be more sympathetic to mulatta characters. Many Chinese-American writers, while undoubtedly aware of the myths surrounding Eurasians in Anglo-American fiction and in the dominant society, chose to ignore the existence of Eurasians in their writings.

Although aspects of Chinese-American history have been neglected by Chinese-American women writers, primary images of Chinese and Chinese-American women in Euro-American fiction remain: prostitution, passivity, and unrelenting evil. Missionary writers and writers for some of the popular magazines published works of fiction that dealt with the position of Chinese women within the Chinese community. Frequently that position was one of subordination and subjection to physical abuse, but the primary image was sexual slave.

These "slave girls" were seldom acknowledged in the writings of Chinese-American women. Sui Sin Far, the first Chinese-American writer, seems to be the only one who directly confronts any part of the early history of Chinese-American women that was considered negative by the dominant culture. The tendency of later Chinese-American women writers seemingly is to ignore any negative experiences of the Chinese in the United States. Peggy Pascoe proposes that "[to] counter these racially-based stereotypes, scholars of Chinese American writing in the 1960s and 1970s tried to desensationalize the Chinese American past by shifting attention away from organized vice."[6] Like African-American women writers prior to Gwendolyn Brooks, many Chinese-American writers countered with "uplift" literature featuring a few upper-class or highly educated women.

At the time, upper-class or well-educated women formed a very small percentage of the women in each group. The majority of the women were trying to survive in an alien, hostile environment. They needed the support of their ethnic group from attacks on their morality from the dominant culture.

Further, those sexual stereotypes represented a form of social control. Most Euro-Americans were immigrants who descended from the peasant class. Once in the United States, many tried to obscure their peasant origins by establishing an identity with the aristocracy, and they saw themselves as superior. As former peasants, they needed a group to which they could feel superior, those visibly different. As a result, a "social etiquette" was instituted to isolate ethnics of color, physically and psychologically, through the use of laws and violence.

Nevertheless, as the African-American stereotype represented the conception of ethnics of color in the South, the Chinese-American stereotype represented the conception of ethnics of color in the West. As degraded as African-American women were in that region and in others as well, so were Chinese-American women, but in a different manner. Chinese-American women were spared some of the images of African-American women. They came to the United States later, and their group had a smaller population, but they still were attacked through their alleged sexuality. Chinese-American women were viewed as helpless Trilbys under the powerful influence of Chinese Svengalis who transformed them into prostitutes in a *de jure* form of slavery. It is improbable that Chinese men could have run this highly profitable business without the collusion of very powerful Euro-Americans, not for lack of intelligence but for a lack of cultural knowledge and the racist laws that would have prevented it. Many Protestant denominations formed groups whose sole purpose was to rescue

these enslaved women. Although these Chinese women possessed reputations as immoral, the general assumption seemed to be that they could be
redeemed if only they could escape their Chinatown brothels. However,
Frank Chin presents a different view of the rescue operations: "Whore-
houses full of Chinese women serving a white-only clientele . . . were
blessed. The aim . . . was to brainwash the Chinese girls against sexual
relations with Chinese men. . . . The bars on the windows . . . were not to
keep Chinese men out, but to keep Chinese women from escaping."[7]

In contrast, many African-American women could not depend on
outsiders to come to their rescue. In the antebellum South, there were some
women like Sarah Grimké who risked punishment to teach slaves. After
Emancipation many Euro-American women went to the South to serve as
teachers to the newly freed slaves. However, by the end of the nineteenth
century with the creation of the brutal African-American rapist image and
increased indictment of the African-American female as lascivious, the
tendency of Euro-Americans to view these images as accurate dried up
much of the charitable support. Therefore, African-American women had
to depend on other African-American women, like educator Nannie Helen
Burroughs or writer Victoria Earle Matthews. Matthews established the
White Rose Mission for Working Women in New York, which eventually
became part of the Urban League. Through their systems of women's
clubs, other African-American women helped their less fortunate sisters
avoid or escape degrading conditions. This is not to deny that there was
financial assistance from Euro-American philanthropists; however, the
condition of Chinese-American prostitutes was seen as somehow different.

Images, positive or negative, are not immutable; they may be altered or
adapted according to a society's needs. The images of Chinese-American
women seemingly have changed. Nevertheless, the contemporary image
of Chinese-American women as members of the "model minority" or
"mascot minority"[8] is at odds with their present-day participation in
sweatshops or low-level positions in the Silicon Valley. This is not the
perspective that is presented in the media. The new "model minority"
stereotype for Asian-Americans is an attempt to rationalize and justify the
continued position of African-Americans as the "pariah minority." The
hyperbole surrounding the stereotype of the "model minority" verifies one
of the oldest American ideals: any racial group can succeed if its members
try hard enough. In its present form, Chinese-Americans and undoubtedly
all Asian-Americans occupy a middleman position between Euro-Americans and African-Americans that validates the power relationships that
exist in this country, thus blaming the victims for their own inequality.

The images of African-American women, on the other hand, have also been revamped. However, changes in the existing social structure in the 1960s were only cosmetic, not revolutionary. The African-American community is still attacked through its women, particularly in the media. Instead of the strident denunciation of the "loose" African-American woman, which was once the norm, there is the voice-over on the evening news speaking of welfare cheats, AIDS, or crack babies; the camera most often zeroes in on an African-American woman. These more contemporary images could well be the updated version of the African-American female.

Unlike African-American writers who were struggling to develop true-to-life characters, Chinese-American women writers after Sui Sin Far, in accentuating their difference and emphasizing their exoticism, began the trend toward the glorification of Chinese culture in which they confirmed many stereotypes. These women writers, primarily Jade Snow Wong, Virginia Lee, and to a lesser extent Amy Tan, seem to be concerned with conforming to the prevalent Euro-American view of their group rather than presenting an accurate although fictional account of the activities of Chinese America. Of course, Wong, Lee, and Tan are not completely representative of their generation or ethnic group. There are silences because of their time period, their ethnicity, and their gender. Factors such as pressure from publishers who purportedly have insisted that the American reading public would not accept writing that did not emphasize the "exoticness" of Chinese life in the United States must be taken into consideration.[9] Still, Han Suyin has written, "Some . . . have achieved fame by pandering to that nostalgic image of a China that never was, save for an infinitesimal number of the elite [they] pander to the superior culture.[10]

Chinese-American women writers seldom confronted racially specific stereotypes. Virginia Lee, the writer of *The House That Tai Ming Built*, for example, has been accused of cultural treachery. That is, she has no first-hand knowledge of Chinese history but has borrowed liberally from European and Euro-American scholars. The Chinese world of which Lee writes is a world in which she probably would not have participated had her family remained in China. The ancestors of most of the Chinese in the United States were from the peasant class rather than the aristocracy. They write of an assumed memory, as Yen Lu Wong avers, "not even a memory of a real past but the memory of a memory . . . for the very old, the way it ought to be. A vague and misty dream . . . clung to in these parts of the diaspora."[11]

But Pascoe's assertion that the avoidance of racially specific stereotypes in Chinese-American writing was an attempt to desensationalize their history is misleading; ignoring history does not obliterate it. Nevertheless, by desensationalizing their history, they more nearly approach "honorary white status." Another reason may be that, similar to many other ethnic groups in this country, they are unaware of their history. But it is the responsibility of the writers to uncover their historical roots and not misrepresent them. Or could it be that their stereotypes were closely allied to African-American stereotypes, and perhaps Chinese-American women writers needed to disassociate themselves from African-Americans.

It would seem that in acknowledging their history in the United States, they would also have to disclose that there had been attempts to "negrocize" them. Not wanting to be identified with African-Americans, with the presumed stigma, degradation, and humiliation of being Black, these writers decided to set their writings in China or in Chinatown. Chinatown, similar to inner-city areas, reflects segregation and the crowding of an ethnic group because of successful discrimination by the dominant group rather than an area selected by the Chinese where their cultural integrity was kept intact. These Chinatowns or ethnic enclaves were ghettos recreated in their writings as aristocratic Chinese mythical areas where supposedly there were no African-Americans present to whom they could be compared.

Both groups were aware of the stereotypes applied to the other. Richard Wright in *Black Boy* suggestively delineates the attitudes of many African-Americans toward Chinese-Americans. Shorty, "the round, yellow, fat elevator boy . . . with the complexion of a Chinese," frequently humiliates himself before Euro-Americans by offering them the opportunity to kick him "in the ass" for twenty-five cents. A passenger, after kicking Shorty, throws him a quarter, which he picks up and puts in his mouth.

Frequently Shorty would threaten to move north. "I'm going north one of these days," Shorty would say.
   We would all laugh, knowing that Shorty would never leave, that he depended too much upon the whites for the food he ate.
   "What would you do up north?" I would ask Shorty.
   "I'd pass for Chinese," Shorty would say.[12]

Wright, in parodying the lengths to which both groups would go for acceptance by Euro-Americans, perhaps overstates his case. But he demonstrates an awareness of the accommodations that Chinese-Americans have made for approval. And Shorty in his Stepin Fechit persona knows, by Southern standards, "his place."

On the other hand, there seems to be no literary awareness of stereotypes assigned to African-Americans in the works of Chinese-American women writers. But if there were a need to disassociate themselves from the negative images of African-Americans, then the absence is understandable. However, there is evidence of the acceptance of the stereotypes among the residents of San Francisco's Chinatown where they united against busing Chinese-American children to African-American inner-city schools. In 1971, the Chinese-Americans filed for an injunction against court-ordered busing. The court denied their petitions, and the Chinese boycotted the public schools. When the schools opened in September 1971, the Chinese-American absentee rate was over 90 percent. Thus, the Chinese-American reaction to busing was the same as Euro-Americans, indicating both an awareness of the negative images and an overidentification with Euro-Americans in their hostility to African-Americans.

Nevertheless, ethnic writers are perceived as spokespersons for their group, and there should be an obligation to truth and accuracy although fictionalized. Much of their writing is accepted because the writer is a member of that group. The cultural "truths" described by Maxine Hong Kingston have been lauded and accepted by non-Chinese-Americans because she is of Chinese heritage and, it is thought, must be knowledgeable of her own culture. In contrast, Kingston has been censured by Chinese-American critics for perpetuating cultural stereotypes, but in varying ways *The Woman Warrior* confronts certain prevailing views, specifically that Chinese-Americans have managed to preserve five thousand years of a cultural integrity or that Confucian precepts foster harmony and respect within the family. Nonetheless, critics have read shades of meaning into Kingston that support their own biased viewpoints. But many of these same critics have ignored many of the "truths" of African-American writing. Alice Walker has been reproached for writing of clitoridectomy in *Possessing the Secret of Joy* because she is not African and presumably cannot understand its cultural significance.

It must be noted that the racial policies of the United States are based on a biracial social system; there are only two races in the country—Black and white—and by failing to deal with the historical racism that has affected Blacks, Chinese-Americans unthinkingly align themselves with Euro-Americans. By reinforcing ties to a Chinese past rather than focusing on an American present or future, Chinese-American women writers do not burden the conscience of their Euro-American readers. They make the readers feel good about themselves.

Both Chinese-American women writers and African-American women writers emphasize strong family ties and acknowledge the special support coming from relationships between women. Chinese-American writers have common threads running through their writing. The principal theme seems to be a preservation of strong cultural traditions. At the same time, they seem unconcerned about broad social issues affecting ethnic communities in the United States.

Toni Morrison's *Beloved*, according to Elizabeth Fox-Genovese, "demonstrates [that] African-American women's fiction can only be understood as the product and reenactment of history, specifically the history of the South and slavery."[13] The experience of slavery is deeply ingrained in the African-American psyche; it is always just beneath the surface of African-American consciousness. Unlike the Chinese-American writers who choose to ignore their history in the United States, African-American women writers have preferred a direct confrontation with their history and the stereotypes that arose from it. Chinese-American women writers have not completed their process of self-definition. They are in a position similar to African-American women writers during the Harlem Renaissance. During the Harlem Renaissance, there was a fascination with African-Americans as exotic primitives. A similar exoticism is present in the writings of many Chinese-American women. Similarly, African-Americans in the Harlem Renaissance wanted to establish cultural authenticity, as do contemporary Chinese-Americans. While African-American writers during this period emphasized their conformity to Euro-American cultural standards, most contemporary Chinese-American writers stress their differences, promoting their foreignness. They do not seem to have evolved at the same rate or in the same manner as African-American women writers. African-American women writers realize the difficulty of survival in a highly complex social structure that is characterized by colorism, sexism, racism, and classism. Chinese-American women writers do not seem to have come to this realization.

NOTES

1. Sui Sin Far, *Mrs. Spring Fragrance* (Chicago: A. C. McClurg, 1912), 220–23.

2. Rosalind Miles, *The Women's History of the World* (New York: Harper and Row, 1989), 242.

3. Bonnie Angelo, "The Pain of Being Black," *Time* (May 22, 1989): 120.

4. Lucy Cheng Hirata, "Free, Indentured, Enslaved: Chinese Prostitution in Nineteenth-Century America," *Signs* (Fall 1979): 104.

5. Ibid., 21.

6. Peggy Pascoe, "Gender Systems in Conflict: The Marriages of Mission-Educated Chinese American Women, 1874–1939," *Journal of Social History* (Summer 1989): 631.

7. Frank Chin et al., eds., *The Big AIIIEEEEE! An Anthology of Chinese American and Japanese American Literature* (New York: Meridian, 1991), 16.

8. Elaine Kim, "Asian Americans and American Popular Culture," in *Dictionary of Asian American History*, Hyung-chan Kim, ed. (Westport, CT: Greenwood Press, 1986), 110.

9. John Paul Eakins, *Fictions in Autobiography: Studies in the Art of Self-Invention* (Princeton, NJ: Princeton University Press, 1985), 165.

10. In Amy Ling, *Between Worlds. Women Writers of Chinese Ancestry* (New York: Pergamon Press, 1990), x.

11. Yen Lu Wong, "Chinese-American Theatre," *Drama* 20 (June 1976): 13.

12. Richard Wright, *Black Boy* (New York: Harper and Row, 1945), 252.

13. Elizabeth Fox-Genovese, "Between Individualism and Fragmentation: American Culture and the New Literary Studies of Race and Gender," *American Quarterly* (March 1990): 16.

Selected Bibliography

This selected bibliography is intended to provide a guide to the critical sources found to be the most useful in conceptualizing and writing this book. Literature that has been treated largely or entirely as primary source material is not included here but is fully listed in the chapter notes.

AFRICAN-AMERICAN

Anderson, Sherwood. *Dark Laughter*. New York: Boni and Liveright, 1925.

Baym, Nina. "The Women of Cooper's Leatherstocking Tales." In *Images of Women in Fiction. Feminist Perspectives*, edited by Susan Koppelman Cornillon, 134–54. Bowling Green, Ohio: Bowling Green University Popular Press, 1973.

Beal, Frances M. " 'Double Jeopardy': To Be Black and Female." In *Sisterhood Is Powerful. An Anthology of Writings from the Women's Liberation Movement,* edited by Robin Morgan, 340–52. New York: Random House, 1970.

_____ . "Slave of a Slave No More. Black Women in Struggle." *Black Scholar* 6 (March 1975): 2–10.

Bell, Bernard W. *The Afro-American Novel and Its Tradition*. Amherst: The University of Massachusetts Press, 1987.

Berzon, Judith R. *White Nor Black. The Mulatto Character in American Fiction*. New York: New York University Press, 1978.

Bishoff, Joan. "The Novels of Toni Morrison. Studies in Thwarted Sensitivity." *Studies in Black Literature* (Fall 1975): 21–23.

Blassingame, John W., ed. *Slave Testimony*. Baton Rouge: Louisiana State University Press, 1977.

Bond, Jean Carey. "The Media Image of Black Women." *Freedomways* (1975): 34–37.

Braithwaite, William Stanley. "The Negro in American Fiction." In *Black Expression,* edited by Addison Gayle, Jr., 169–81. New York: Weybright and Talley, 1969.

Brown, Sterling. "Negro Character as Seen by White Authors." In *Dark Symphony. Negro Literature in America,* edited by James A. Emmanuel and Theodore L. Gross, 139–71. New York: The Free Press, 1968.

Bullock, Penelope. "The Mulatto in American Fiction." *Phylon* 6 (1945): 78–82.

Cable, George W. *The Grandissimes.* New York: American Century Series, 1957.

Cade, Toni. *The Black Woman.* New York: New American Library, 1970.

Carby, Hazel. *Reconstructing Womanhood. The Emergence of the Afro-American Woman Novelist.* New York: Oxford University Press, 1987.

Chopin, Kate. *Bayou Folk.* Ridgewood, NJ: The Gregg Press, 1967 (1894).

Christian, Barbara. *Black Women Novelists. The Development of a Tradition, 1892–1976.* Westport, CT: Greenwood Press, 1980.

Duster, Alfreda M., ed. *Crusade for Justice: The Autobiography of Ida B. Wells.* Chicago: The University of Chicago Press, 1970.

Eckley, Wilton. *T. S. Stribling.* Boston: Twayne Publishers, 1975.

Fiedler, Leslie A. *Love and Death in the American Novel.* New York: Stein and Day, 1966.

Frings, Ketti. *Look Homeward, Angel. A Play.* New York: Charles Scribner's Sons, 1958.

Gross, Seymour L., and John Edward Hardy, eds. *Images of the Negro in American Literature.* Chicago: The University of Chicago Press, 1966.

Harris, Trudier. *From Mammies to Militants. Domestics in Black American Literature.* Philadelphia: Temple University Press, 1982.

Hemenway, Robert. *Zora Neale Hurston. A Literary Biography.* Urbana: The University of Illinois Press, 1978.

Holloway, Karla, and Stephanie A. Demetrakopoulos. *New Dimensions of Spirituality. A Biracial and Bicultural Reading of the Novels of Toni Morrison.* Westport, CT: Greenwood Press, 1987.

Kapai, Leela. "Dominant Themes and Techniques in Paule Marshall's Fiction." *CLA Journal* 16 (September 1972): 49–59.

Larsen, Nella. *Passing.* New York: Arno Press and The New York Times, 1969 (1929).

McKay, Nellie Y., ed. *Critical Essays on Toni Morrison.* Boston: G. K. Hall and Co., 1988.

Meeker, Richard K., ed. *The Collected Stories of Ellen Glasgow.* Baton Rouge: Louisiana State University Press, 1963.

Nelson, John Herbert. *The Negro Character in American Literature.* College Park, MD: McGrath Publishing Co., 1926.

Page, Sally R. *Faulkner's Women. Characterization and Meaning.* De Land, FL: Everett/Edwards, Inc., 1972.

Peterkin, Julia. *Scarlet Sister Mary*. Indianapolis: The Bobbs-Merrill Co., 1928.

Peters, Erskin. *William Faulkner: The Yoknapatawpha World and Black Being*. Darby, PA: Norwood Editions, 1984.

Riggins, Ann L. "The Works of Frances E. W. Harper." *Black World* (December 1972): 30–37.

Sadoff, Dianne F. "Black Matrilineage. The Case of Alice Walker and Zora Neale Hurston." *Signs: Journal of Women in Society* 2 (Autumn 1985): 4–26.

Shockely, Ann Allen. "Pauline Elizabeth Hopkins. A Biographical Excursion into Obscurity." *Phylon* (Spring 1972): 22–26.

Stone, Pauline Terrelonge. "Feminist Consciousness and Black Women." In *Women. A Feminist Perspective,* Jo Freeman, ed. Palo Alto, CA: Mayfield Publishing Co., 1979.

Tate, Claudia. "Pauline Hopkins: Our Literary Foremother." In *Conjuring. Black Women, Fiction and Literary Tradition,* Marjorie Pryse and Hortense J. Spillers, eds. Bloomington: Indiana University Press, 1985.

Twain, Mark. *Pudd' nhead Wilson*. New York: Harcourt, Brace and World, Inc., 1894.

Van Deburg, William L. *Slavery and Race in American Culture*. Madison: The University of Wisconsin Press, 1984.

Warren, Robert Penn. *Brothers to Dragons. A Tale in Verse and Voices*. New York: Random House, 1953.

Wells-Barnett, Ida B. *On Lynchings*. New York: Arno Press and The New York Times, 1969.

Williamson, Joel. *New People. Miscegenation and Mulattoes in the United States*. New York: The Free Press, 1980.

Willis, Susan. *Specifying. Black Women Writing the American Experience*. Madison: The University of Wisconsin Press, 1987.

Wright, Sarah E. "The Negro Woman in American Literature." *Freedomways* 6 (Winter 1966): 8–25.

Yarborough, Richard. "The Quest for the American Dream in Three Afro-American Novels: *If He Hollers Let Him Go, The Street,* and *Invisible Man*." *MELUS* 8 (Winter 1981): 33–59.

Yellin, Jean Fagin. *The Intricate Knot. Black Figures in American Literature, 1776–1863*. New York: New York University Press, 1972.

Youman, Mary Mabel. "Nella Larsen's *Passing*: A Study in Irony." *CLA Journal* (December 1974): 235–41.

CHINESE-AMERICAN

Baker, Houston A., ed. *Three American Literatures. Essays in Chicano, Native American and Asian-American Literature*. New York: The Modern Language Association of America, 1982.

Barnhart, Josephine Baker. *The Fair But Frail. Prostitution in San Francisco: 1849–1900*. Reno: The University of Nevada Press, 1986.

Blinde, Patricia Lin. "The Icicle in the Desert: Perspective and Form in the Works of Two Chinese-American Women Writers." *MELUS* 6 (1979): 51–57.

Butcher, Phillip, ed. *The Ethnic Image in Modern American Literature: 1900–1950*. Volume 1. Washington, D.C.: Howard University Press, 1984.

Carlson, Lewis H., and George A. Colburn. *In Their Place. White America Defines Her Minorities, 1850–1950*. New York: John Wiley and Sons, 1972.

Chua, Chen Lok. "Two Versions of the American Dream. The Gold Mountain in Lin Yutang and Maxine Hong Kingston." *MELUS* 8 (1981): 61–70.

Clark, Helen F. *The Lady of the Lily Feet*. Philadelphia: The Griffith and Rowland Press, 1900.

Confucius. *The Great Digest. The Unwobbling Pivot. The Analects*. Trans. Ezra Pound. New York: New Directions Books, 1969.

Coolidge, Mary Roberts. *Chinese Immigration*. New York: Arno Press and The New York Times, 1969 (1900).

Daniels, Roger, and Harry H. L. Kitano. *American Racism. Exploration of the Nature of Prejudice*. Englewood Cliffs, NJ: Prentice-Hall, Inc., 1970.

Hirata, Lucie Cheng. "Chinese Immigrant Women in Nineteenth Century California." In *Asian and Pacific American Experiences,* Nobuya Tsuchida, ed. Minneapolis: Asian/Pacific American Learning Resource Center, 1972.

Isaacs, Harold R. *Images of Asia. American Views of China and India*. New York: Capricorn Books, 1958.

Keim, Margaret Laton. "The Chinese as Portrayed in the Works of Bret Harte: A Study of Race Relations." *Sociology and Social Research* 25 (1941): 441–50.

Kim, Elaine. *Asian American Literature. An Introduction to the Writings and Their Social Context*. Philadelphia: Temple University Press, 1982.

Levy, Howard. *Chinese Footbinding. The History of A Curious Erotic Custom*. New York: Walter Rawls, 1968.

Ling, Amy. "A Perspective on Chinamerican Literature." *MELUS* 8 (1981): 76–81.

———. "A Rumble in the Silence: *Crossings* by Chuang Hua." *MELUS* 9 (1982): 29–37.

———. "Edith Eaton: Pioneer Chinamerican Writer and Feminist." *American Literary Realism. 1870–1910* (1983): 287–96.

———. "Winnifred Eaton: Ethnic Chameleon and Popular Success." *MELUS* 11 (1984): 5–15.

———. "Writers with a Cause: Sui Sin Far and Han Suyin." *Women's Studies International Forum* 9 (1986): 411–19.

Martin, Mildred Crowl. *Chinatown's Angry Angel. The Story of Donaldina Cameron*. Palo Alto, CA: Pacific Books Publishers, 1977.

Rabine, Leslie W. "No Lost Paradise: Social Gender and Symbolic Gender in the Writings of Maxine Hong Kingston." *Signs: Journal of Women in Society* 12:3 (1987): 471–92.

Seller, Maxine Schwartz, ed. *Immigrant Women*. Philadelphia: Temple University Press, 1981.

Smith, Sidonie. *A Poetics of Women's Autobiography. Marginality and the Fictions of Self-Representation*. Bloomington: Indiana University Press, 1987.

Social Science Institute. *Orientals and Their Cultural Adjustment*. Social Science Source Document No. 4. Nashville: Fisk University, 1946.

Spoehr, Luther W. "Sambo and the Heathen Chinee: Californians' Racial Stereotypes in the Late 1870s." *Pacific Historical Review* 42 (May 1973): 185–204.

Sue, Stanley, and Nathaniel N. Wagner, eds. *Asian American Psychological Perspectives*. Ben Lomond, CA: Science and Behavior Books, 1973.

Swee, Kathleen Loh, and Kristoffer F. Paulson. "The Divided Voice of Chinese-American Narration: Jade Snow Wong's *Fifth Chinese Daughter*." *MELUS* 9 (1982): 53–59.

Tachiki, Amy, et al., eds. *Roots. An Asian American Reader*. Los Angeles: UCLA Asian-American Studies Center, 1971.

Telemaque, Eleanor Wong. *It's Crazy to Stay Chinese in Minnesota*. New York: Thomas Nelson, 1978.

Wang, Veronica. "Reality and Fantasy. The Chinese-American Woman's Quest for Identity." *MELUS* 12 (1985): 23–31.

Wayne, Charles Miller. "Cultural Consciousness in a Multi-Cultural Society: The Uses of Literature." *MELUS* 8 (1981): 29–44.

Wong, Eugene Franklin. *On Visual Media Racism. Asians in American Motion Pictures*. New York: Arno Press, 1978.

Wong, Jade Snow. *No Chinese Stranger*. New York: Harper, 1975.

Wu, William. *The Yellow Peril*. Hamden, CT: Archon Books, 1986.

Index

DuBois, W.E.B., 36, 52

Eat a Bowl of Tea, 97–99, 113
Eaton, Edith. *See* Sui Sin Far
Eaton, Winnifred (Onoto Watanna), 114
Eurasian, 109, 118, 140

Faulkner, William, 35–36
Fifth Chinese Daughter, 115–17
"Food for All His Dead," 100
The Frontiers of Love, 118–21
Fu Manchu, 93

Giddings, Paula, 9, 30
Go Down, Moses, 35
Grant, Ulysses S., 9
Green, Paul, 32
Gutman, Herbert, 34

Hammett, Dashiell, 92
Han Suyin, 128, 143
Harper, Frances, 53
Harte, Bret, 87, 106 n.19
"The Haunted Valley," 88
Helper, Hinton, 4
Hergesheimer, Joseph, 91
Heywood, Dorothy, 30
Heywood, DuBose, 30
Hildredth, Richard, 23
Hopkins, Pauline, 54
The House That Tai Ming Built, 117–18
Howells, William Dean, 26
Hughes, Langston, 70
Hurston, Zora Neale, 59, 70

An Imperative Duty, 26–28
Incidents in the Life of a Slave Girl, Written by Herself, 50–51
In Love and Trouble, 70–73
Iola Leroy, 53–54

"Jackrabbit," 99

Jacobs, Harriet Ann (Linda Brent), 50
Java Head, 91–92
Jefferson, Thomas, 21
The Joy Luck Club, 126–28

Kearney, Dennis, 8, 16 n.43, 83
Kingston, Maxine Hong, 69, 123

La China Poblana, 2
The Land of Gold, 4
Larsen, Nella, 56
The Last of the Mohicans, 21–22
Lee, Virginia Chin-lan, 117, 143
Lerner, Gerda, 29, 37
Ling, Amy, 118, 123
Loose women, 21, 28–29, 137
Lynching, 51–52

McCullers, Carson, 38
Mamba's Daughters, 31–32
Mammy. *See* Aunt Jemima
Marshall, Paule, 65
Matriarchy, 29
Maude Martha, 64, 138
The Member of the Wedding, 38
"Middle Passage," 4, 13
Miller, Stuart C., 4, 82
"Model minority," 101, 142
Morrison, Toni, 67, 124
Mrs. Spring Fragrance, 110–14, 135
Mulatta, 21, 22, 26, 28, 42 nn.13, 14, 51, 58, 76 n.42, 137, 138

No Chinese Stranger, 117

"The Old Order," 37
Our Nig, 48–50
Overland Monthly, 88, 89

Page Law, 9, 115 n.9
The Peculiar Institution, 8
People v. Hall, 6
Petry, Ann, 62

About the Author

MARY E. YOUNG is Assistant Professor of English and Black Studies at The College of Wooster, Wooster, Ohio.